Every Eye Shall See Him!

*A Scriptural Examination
of Christian Doctrines
Related to the Great Tribulation,
the Second Coming of Christ,
and the Rapture of the Church*

Daniel T. Gilmore

Scripture quotations are from the
King James Version.

Self Published © Copyright 2007
Charlevoix, Michigan
All Rights Reserved

ISBN: 978-0-6151-7463-1

This book is dedicated to the glory of my
Lord and Savior Jesus Christ,
and to the praise and honor of His holy name.

I also affectionately dedicate this work
to my dearest friend and life partner, Jackie.
Her unfailing love gives me inspiration
for each new day.

Contents:

Acknowledgments v
Forward vi
Introduction: Definition of Terms x

PART I - THE CHURCH'S PURIFYING HOPE 1
   1: A Meeting in the Air 3
   2: A Thief in the Night 16
   3: In the Twinkling of an Eye 22
   4: Looking for an Escape 26
   5: Will There Be Two Second Comings of Christ? 36
   6: Are the Redeemed Appointed to Wrath? 42
   7: Sealing the Saints of God 50
   8: A Restrainer of Evil Is Removed 61
   9: That Great Gettin' Up Mornin' 66
  10: Thoughts on Imminence 71
  11: The Church and Redeemed Israel 79
  12: Excluding the Olivet Discourse 87
  13: The Secret Rapture Theory 93
  14: The "Mystery Doctrine" Defense 100
  15: Christ's Appearing 106
  16: General Observations 110

PART II - SIGNS OF HIS SOON RETURN 114
  17: Israel's Gathering and Salvation 115
  18: Technology and Travel Rapidly Increase 121
  19: Wars and International Crises 124
  20: Increase of Natural Calamities 127
  21: Christians Hated of All Nations 129
  22: False Christs and False Prophets Abound 133
  23: Iniquity Abounds and Love Diminishes 136
  24: The Gospel Preached in All the World 143
  25: The Great Apostasy 145
  26: A One-World Religion and Government 148
  27: Revealing of the Antichrist 151
  28: A Rebuilt Temple 156
  29: Abomination of Desolation 159
  30: Mark of the Beast 162
  31: Scoffers 164
  32: Conclusion 169

Appendix A: Israel's Restoration 171
Bibliography 175
General Index: 176
Scripture Index: 177

Acknowledgments

Listing by name all the people whom I know have contributed to this work would cover several pages. The list would include several pastors, teachers, and friends who have been used of the Lord to instill within my heart a love for God's Word and a realization of the relevance of Scripture for daily living.

In particular though, and in loving memory, I would like to acknowledge my mother, Barbara. She had a contagious love for the Lord and His Word. This is a blessed spiritual heritage and I rejoice in it. Among my earliest recollections are those times of sitting in church beside my dear mother. By her faithful and loving witness I knew that I needed the blood atonement of Jesus Christ. For that reason alone, I am eternally in her debt.

I also want to acknowledge the help and reassurance that I have received from my friend, Ron Willey, and to extend to him my heartfelt thanks. His gentle urgings and timely assistance are largely responsible for this book going to print. I am grateful for his technical advice and even more for his brotherly encouragement.

Forward

Dear Reader;

Greetings! *Grace and peace be multiplied unto you through the knowledge of God, and of Jesus our Lord, According as his divine power hath given unto us all things that pertain unto life and godliness, through the knowledge of him that hath called us to glory and virtue.*[a]

As you read this, I encourage you to take advantage of a special promise given to the child of God: *If any of you lack wisdom, let him ask of God, that giveth to all men liberally, and upbraideth not; and it shall be given him. But let him ask in faith, nothing wavering. For he that wavereth is like a wave of the sea driven with the wind and tossed.*[b]

I have come to greatly value this precious promise, since I am in daily need of its provisions. Please recognize, though, that a primary component of asking in faith is that we believe God has the right answers and we genuinely want to receive them from Him. In other words it means asking with a mind ready to learn and a heart ready to obey. Please read this book with a sincere desire to know the truth and to live therein, with the goal of promoting the ministry of reconciliation.

The title of this book (Every Eye Shall See Him!) is taken from Revelation 1:7, and this phrase expresses what I believe to be one of the most vital truths that the Church of Christ should affirm about the Lord's return. Though there are many today who teach that there will be a secretive coming of Christ to receive His bride, my reading of scripture contends for an understanding that Christ's return will be evident to all men, believer and unbeliever alike. The sense is that if anyone is in doubt as to whether it is Christ then it is not Christ.

---

a 2 Peter 1:2-3.

b James 1:5-6.

As you read through the following pages I trust that you will be driven to Bible study. Evidenced by the extensive Scripture index at the back of this book, I have attempted to lay out the Word of God for a careful and prayerful examination. If this study aids you in searching the Scriptures then my primary goals for writing this book have been realized. The Word of God alone is the *lamp unto* [our] *feet, and a light unto* [our] *path.*[a] Therefore, my desire is that you study the following pages with Berean nobility!

Without question, there is considerable debate and disagreement among Christians regarding the details of the return of Christ. Also, and too often, there have been deep contentions in the body of Christ over the doctrines of the second coming. These disputes are a source of grief to Christians, and to their Lord. I in no way want to add fuel to this divisiveness. God has called His Church unto unity, and we should always work to promote *the unity of the Spirit in the bond of peace.*[b] Indeed, in putting forth this writing my desire is to do just that.

This unity, of course, only comes from the truth, as the Lord Jesus has said: *If ye continue in my word, then are ye my disciples indeed; And ye shall know the truth, and the truth shall make you free.*[c] Christians understand that our first and final authority on matters of doctrine is the Word of God. Thus, as noted, I have attempted to simply present many of the eschatological texts of Scripture to the reader for a detailed and prayerful examination. Doubtless, God will promote the truth as we give heed to His Word.

The majority of this volume is dedicated to identifying and critiquing what I believe to be Scripturally unsupported teachings about the return of Christ. My critique will, assuredly, be quite pointed at times. So please let this be understood at the outset, I believe that those who concern themselves with questions of this nature love the Lord and His Word, they *love his appearing*[d] and are looking forward to it. All

---

a Psalm 119:105.

b Ephesians 4:3.

c John 8:31-32.

d 2 Timothy 4:8.

who hold such affections are considered by me to be beloved brethren. There is certainly no desire on my part to aid the enemy in his evil work of sowing discord among brethren.[a] Rather, my prayer is that *we all come in the unity of the faith, and of the knowledge of the Son of God, unto a perfect man, unto the measure of the stature of the fulness of Christ.*[b]

Be assured that in differing with some over their interpretation of eschatology and the apocalypse, issue is taken with the teaching, not the teacher. In none of the teachings about Christ's return which are at issue in this book, do I suppose the proponents of other views to be unbelievers or even unspiritual believers. Quite the contrary, I firmly believe that those Christians who seek God's truth on these matters are among those most vitally connected to Christ and His Word.

I believe that God fearing Christians holding differences in understanding on the meaning of eschatological texts is a temporal reality for believers in Christ Jesus. All believers who are on this side of glory testify that *we know in part, and we prophesy in part.*[c] This is true because *now we see through a glass, darkly; but then face to face: now* [we] *know in part; but then shall* [we] *know even as also* [we are] *known.*[d]

Therefore, let me clearly affirm my belief that to de-Christianize or de-spiritualize believers who hold opposing views on these matters is not only uncharitable, it is also grave presumption. He who presumes to hold perfect understanding on these matters denies the reality of the previous texts which affirm otherwise, and is, at best, himself deluded. Certainly matters of doctrine pertaining to the second coming of Christ, like all matters of Christian doctrine, are vitally important and precious. And we indeed must *earnestly contend for the faith which was once delivered unto the saints.*[e] But this contending for the faith must be

---

a See Proverbs 6:14, 19.

b Ephesians 4:13.

c 1 Corinthians 13:9.

d 1 Corinthians 13:12.

e Jude 1:3.

done in love, especially among Christian brethren. Unfortunately, it seems that the grave importance of these issues can, and often does, cause godly men to become over zealous for the truth as they see it, and thereby wound the spirits of other Christian brethren. Every care should be given to avoid this grief, and I have earnestly sought to do just that.

For the sake of clarity, the following is the groundwork of doctrine that underlies this book. In relation to our Lord Jesus Christ's return, I believe in the premillennial, bodily return of Jesus Christ, and in the physical resurrection of the saints and Rapture of the Church at that second coming. I believe that the second coming of Christ, including the Rapture of the Church, will occur after a prophesied literal seven year period of time which will include great tribulation. By definition that makes me a posttribulationist. It is also my understanding that many of the Messianic[a] and eschatological prophecies of both the Old and New Testaments are still future. I believe that each of these doctrines, as with all Christian doctrines, are to rest solely upon the authority of the inerrant, infallible Word of God.

May the Lord truly bless your life, guiding you into all truth as it is in Jesus Christ. This book is dedicated to Christ's glory and to the praise of His holy name. May the Holy Ghost's anointing commend His truth to the hearts of His beloved Church. ***Now unto him that is able to keep you from falling, and to present you faultless before the presence of his glory with exceeding joy, To the only wise God our Saviour, be glory and majesty, dominion and power, both now and for ever. Amen.[b]***

---

a Future as to the Messiah's second coming. The Lord Christ Jesus is the Messiah of Israel and the Savior of the world, and many Old Testament prophecies have already been fulfilled in Christ's first advent. Many more, however, will not be completely fulfilled until His second advent.

b Jude 1:24-25.

Introduction: **Definition of Terms**

Eschatology

Eschatology means, *The doctrine of the last or final things, as death, resurrection, immortality, the end of the age, the second advent of Christ, judgment, and the future state.*[a]　Its particular theological definition is chiefly related to doctrines of the return of Christ. The word is derived from the Greek, *eschatos* (ἔσχατος), meaning *ends of, last, latter end, lowest, uttermost.*[b]　Therefore, a Scriptural study in *eschatology* is primarily concerned with the Biblical prophecies pertaining to the second coming of Christ and the end of the world.

Apocalypse

Apocalypse means *revelation*. Here is the definition as rendered by Webster: *1. [cap.] The last book of the New Testament, otherwise called* The Revelation of St. John the Divine. *2. Any writing professing to reveal the future; esp., such a writing in early Christian circles or, in Jewish circles, between about 200 B.C. and 100 A.D. 3. Anything viewed as a revelation; a disclosure.*[c]　The word is from the Greek, *apokalupsis* (ἀποκάλυψις), meaning *disclosure: –appearing, coming, lighten, manifestation, be revealed, revelation.*[d]

The Great Tribulation

The phrase, *Great Tribulation*, is the descriptive designation that the Lord Jesus used to classify a time of great trouble and calamity that

---

a Webster's New International Dictionary, pg. 871.

b James Strong, The Greek Dictionary of the NT, pg. 33, #2078.

c Webster's New International Dictionary, pg. 125.

d James Strong, The Greek Dictionary of the NT, pg. 14, #602.

will come upon the inhabitants of the earth just prior to the His return. This trouble will intensify to previously unknown dimensions after an event described as ***the abomination of desolation.***[a] This time of trouble will include cataclysmic natural and man-made disasters,[b] intensified satanic and demonic activity,[c] devastating persecution and martyrdom of believers,[d] and judgments from God.

The Lord instructed His disciples that at the time of the end there will ***be <u>great tribulation</u>, such as was not since the beginning of the world to this time, no, nor ever shall be.***[e] A number of Old and New Testament prophetic writings foretell of this time of world wide tribulation or trouble. Specifically the books of Daniel[f] and Revelation[g] establish that this time of trouble will be a seven year span of time divided into two 3½ year periods, the last of which will be the period of Great Tribulation.

The Rapture of the Church

The term, *Rapture*, here refers to the translation of the Church from this world and into the presence of Christ Jesus at His second coming. Though the word is not used in Scripture, one definition of *Rapture* is *to be transported with joy.*[h] Therefore, it is a good word to describe this prophesied *catching up* of the Church. The Bible reveals that there will be a *Rapture* of the Church at the return of the Lord Jesus Christ. At the Rapture of the Church the saints of God which have passed away

---

a Matthew 24:15. See Chapter 29 for a specific examination of this sign.

b See Matthew 24:7, Luke 21:11, 25-26, & Revelation 6:3-8, 12-14.

c See Revelation 12:12-13, 13:1-8.

d See Matthew 24:9, Luke 21:12, & Revelation 6:9-11.

e Matthew 24:21.

f One "week" of years divided in half: see Daniel 9:27, the second 3½ year period being after the abomination of desolation: see Daniel 12:7.

g Two 1,260 day periods: see Revelation 11:3, 12:6. Two forty two month periods: see Revelation 11:2, 13:5.

h <u>Webster's New International Dictionary</u>, p. 2063.

(*which are fallen asleep*[a]) will be resurrected, and they, with the living saints, will be instantaneously glorified[b] and *caught up... in the clouds to meet the Lord in the air.*[c] The Rapture of the Church is the culminating event of redemption. At the Rapture of the Church the threefold aspect of redemption will be fully realized; for the justification, sanctification, and glorification of the redeemed will be completed on that glorious morning. This then is the great and purifying hope of the Church. *And every man that hath this hope in him purifieth himself, even as he is pure.*[d]

Various Rapture Viewpoints

Since some believe that the Rapture of the Church is separated from the second coming of Christ by a span of time, it should be remembered that the prefixes *"pre"* and *"post"* in the following two italicized terms refer to the timing of the Rapture and not necessarily to the timing of Christ's second coming.

The term, *pretribulationism,* identifies the belief that the Rapture of the Church will occur before the Great Tribulation of the last days. From this eschatological viewpoint the Rapture of the Church will precede the second coming of Christ by a span of time, usually understood to be at least seven years in length. Pretribulationists teach that between the Rapture of the Church and the return of Christ there will be a time of great tribulation on the earth. The pretribulationist believes that the Church will be in heaven with Christ during the Great Tribulation.

The term, *posttribulationism,* identifies the belief that the Rapture of the Church will occur after the Great Tribulation of the last days. From this eschatological viewpoint the Rapture of the Church will occur

---

a 1 Thessalonians 4:15.

b See 1 Corinthians 15:51-54.

c 1 Thessalonians 4:17.

d 1 John 3:3.

at the second coming of Christ and is a primary reason for His return. Posttribulationists teach that there will be great tribulation on the earth before Christ's return which the living Church of Christ will endure.

There are other viewpoints as to the timing of the Rapture, such as *midtribulationism* and *pre-wrath Rapture*. These other viewpoints will not specifically be critiqued in this volume. However, both of these viewpoints also place a time-separation between the Rapture of the Church and the second coming of Christ. Therefore, at least in that respect, they are similar to pretribulationism.

Millennial Views

The term, *millennium,* means one-thousand years. There are three basic viewpoints with reference to the prophesied one-thousand year reign of Christ on earth. (*And I saw thrones, and they sat upon them, and judgment was given unto them: and I saw the souls of them that were beheaded for the witness of Jesus, and for the word of God, and which had not worshipped the beast, neither his image, neither had received his mark upon their foreheads, or in their hands; and they lived and reigned with Christ a thousand years. But the rest of the dead lived not again until the thousand years were finished. This is the first resurrection. Blessed and holy is he that hath part in the first resurrection: on such the second death hath no power, but they shall be priests of God and of Christ, and shall reign with him a thousand years.*[a])

Premillennialism. This position generally holds that this *thousand years* reign of Christ will be a literal period of time established by Christ and commencing with His second advent. During this reign Christ will remove sin's curse from the earth and it will be an unparalleled time of peace, health, bounty, and delight on earth.

Postmillennialism. This position generally holds that this *thousand years* reign of Christ is a figurative period of time referring to a time of

---

a Revelation 20:4-6.

peace and blessing on earth that will be established by the Church of Jesus Christ prior to Christ's return and will come to completion at His return.

Amillennialism. This position generally holds that Scriptural references to this ***thousand years*** reign of Christ are figurative or allegorical references to Christ's Lordship over the Church age as a whole, and thus, there will be no actual one-thousand year reign of Christ on earth.

I consider the *premillennial viewpoint* to be the settled doctrine of the eschatological texts of Scripture. However, millennial viewpoints are not the focus of this work and will not be critiqued in any specific manner herein.

Nevertheless, as an intriguing aside, it may be instructive to some to consider that according to Biblical chronology the year AD 2000 marks approximately the six-thousandth year of human history. If man is indeed in the very last days before the return of Christ, then the millennial reign would begin around the beginning of the seventh millennium of the earth. That six-to-one ratio corresponds in an interesting way to the six days of creation and the seventh day of rest. The possible parallel between the two may even be alluded to in a declaration made by the Apostle Peter: ***one day is with the Lord as a thousand years, and a thousand years as one day.***[a] This would make earth's seventh millennium the millennium of rest. In that time, Christ will reign, the curse of sin will fail, and God's grace and glory will prevail.

---

a 2 Peter 3:8; see also, Psalm 90:4.

PART I
THE CHURCH'S PURIFYING HOPE

The promise of Christ's return is called the purifying hope of the Church. The knowledge that Christ will return in righteousness to receive His holy bride and then meet out judgment to all mankind, is to be a great holy flame that burns in the heart of the Christian. John the Apostle gave this hallowed instruction to the Church of Jesus Christ: *Beloved, now are we the sons of God, and it doth not yet appear what we shall be: but we know that, when he shall appear, we shall be like him; for we shall see him as he is. And every man that hath this hope in him purifieth himself, even as he is pure.*[a]

In the following chapters the promise of Christ's return, or this purifying hope of the Church, will be studied. There are many instructions in God's Word about the Lord's second coming that are precise as to both what we should believe and what we should do. These directions are left for the Church so that she will not only wait for her Lord expectantly, but also confidently. Christ's Church must hold a purpose of heart to know all the things that her Lord has left for her to know. And, as with all matters of redemption, the Christian must seek to hear only one voice on this matter, the voice of her Lord.

There are many things with regard to Christ's second advent that are uncertain and some things that are decidedly not for the Church to know. Nevertheless, many precise instructions about Christ's return have been given in God's Word. God has given a holy task to His Church. She is to seek out these teachings about Christ's return and live by the imperatives of these teachings. Christians are also directed to tell others about these truths.

With the purifying hope of Christ's return before her eyes, the Church's holy purpose in living and working should be summed up in the words of the Apostle Paul: *I count all things but loss for the*

---

a 1 John 3:2-3.

excellency of the knowledge of Christ Jesus my Lord: for whom I have suffered the loss of all things, and do count them but dung, that I may win Christ, And be found in him, not having mine own righteousness, which is of the law, but that which is through the faith of Christ, the righteousness which is of God by faith.[a]

In the preparative directives that the Lord has given in His Word, a consistent theme emerges. Namely, that the season of Christ's coming for His bride will include a trouble, travail, or tribulation for that bride. This travail, trouble, or tribulation is defined as being both physical and spiritual.   Physically, Christians are directed to prepare for the persecutions and hardships which will precede Christ's return. Spiritually, Christians are directed to live in a state of readiness to meet the Lord and to prepare for deceptions and heresies that will proliferate to epic proportions just before the Lord's return.

God has intended that the holy flame of the blessed hope of the Church be that which keeps her in watchful readiness for the great and glorious day of the Lord Jesus Christ. Christians are accountable to watch for their Lord's return. The Lord gave the doctrines and signs of His return so that His bride would be instructed, warned, admonished, and encouraged. In the pages that follow many of these signs and directives will be examined. May the Lord bless each reader with spiritual insight to discern how to live, and watch, and prepare for *the great and the terrible day of the LORD.*[b]

---

a Philippians 3:8-9.

b Joel 2:31.

1:   A Meeting in the Air

Included below are several passages that describe the Rapture or *catching up* of the Church.   Comprised in these references are the primary Scriptural declarations about the Rapture.   These texts confirm that at the return of Christ, the saints which have died in the faith will be resurrected, and they, with the living saints, will be *caught up... in the clouds, to meet the Lord in the air.*[a]   This redemptive event will be ministered by the angels of heaven; for the Bible declares that *the angels shall gather together his elect from the four winds, from the uttermost part of the earth to the uttermost part of heaven.*[b]   Also at the Rapture of the Church the instantaneous glorification of the all the redeemed will occur, *For this corruptible must put on incorruption, and this mortal must put on immortality.*[c]

The Bible states with reference to timing, that the blessed Rapture of the Church and the instantaneous glorification of the redeemed will take place when the people of the earth actually *see the Son of man coming in the clouds of heaven with power and great glory.*[d]   And the trumpet call that will announce the Rapture of the Church will be *the last trump.*[e]

Texts Disclosing the Time Line of the Rapture

Matthew 24:29-31 - [29]Immediately after the tribulation of those days shall the sun be darkened, and the moon shall not give her light, and the stars shall fall from heaven, and the powers of the heavens shall be shaken: [30]And then shall appear the sign of the Son of man in heaven: and then shall all the tribes of the earth

---

a 1 Thessalonians 4:17.

b Matthew 13:25.

c 1 Corinthians 15:54.

d Matthew 24:30.

e 1 Corinthians 15:52.

mourn, and they shall see the Son of man coming in the clouds of heaven with power and great glory. [31]And he shall send his angels with a great sound of a trumpet, and they shall gather together his elect from the four winds, from one end of heaven to the other.

Mark 13:24-27 - [24]But in those days, after that tribulation, the sun shall be darkened, and the moon shall not give her light, [25]And the stars of heaven shall fall, and the powers that are in heaven shall be shaken. [26]And then shall they see the Son of man coming in the clouds with great power and glory. [27]And then shall he send his angels, and shall gather together his elect from the four winds, from the uttermost part of the earth to the uttermost part of heaven.

These two texts give the clearest time line in Scripture of the events surrounding the return of Christ and the Rapture of the Church. It is unquestionably clear from these passages that the gathering of the elect[a] in the air happens *Immediately after the tribulation of those days.*[b] Notice that the timing is stated quite plainly to be: *after that tribulation.*[c] The Bible declares that Christ will come in the clouds and *send his angels with a great sound of a trumpet, and they shall gather together his elect from the four winds, from one end of heaven to the other.*[d] The Gospel of Mark states it this way: *then shall he send his angels, and shall gather together his elect from the four winds, from the uttermost part of the earth to the uttermost part of heaven.*[e] The plain understanding that Christ will return and gather the elect of the earth to Himself after the Great Tribulation of those days is the obvious message here.

---

a These are born-again believers. See the following texts where *elect* is used to describe the Church: Romans 8:33, Colossians 3:12, Titus 1:1, 1 Peter 1:2, & 1 John 1:1, 13.

b Matthew 24:29.

c Mark 13:24.

d Matthew 24:31.

e Mark 13:27.

These clear time-sequenced proclamations confirm that living disciples of the Lord*a* will experience the"Great Tribulation" spoken of in these texts, and they will find blessed deliverance by Christ *Immediately after the tribulation of those days.*[b] This deliverance is said to come at the time that Christ Jesus is actually seen coming *in the clouds of heaven with power and great glory.*[c] Only by overlooking, contorting, or arbitrarily cutting apart these texts*d* can any other meaning emerge. Please notice that Jesus is revealing the time line of these great events. Throughout the Olivet Discourse (Matthew 24-25, Mark 13, and Luke 21,) Christ distinctly used phrases like, *then shall,* and *immediately after.* Thus, He placed these events in a precise time sequence which He then clearly unfolded to His disciples.

The "Taken and Left" Reference

Matthew 24:38-41 - *³⁸For as in the days that were before the flood they were eating and drinking, marrying and giving in marriage, until the day that Noe entered into the ark, ³⁹And knew not until the flood came, and <u>took</u> them all away; so shall also the coming of the Son of man be. ⁴⁰Then shall two be in the field; the one shall be <u>taken</u>, and the other left. ⁴¹Two women shall be grinding at the mill; the one shall be <u>taken</u>, and the other left.*[e]

There is some question as to what the *taken* of these verses is referring to. Some believe this passage speaks of being taken in judgment, still others believe it means being taken up in the Rapture. The *took* of verse 39 is clearly a taking into judgment. However,

---

a This assuredly means Christians, therefore, Christian believers will be alive and on earth at that time.

b Matthew 24:29.

c Matthew 24:30.

d Please see chapter 12 for an examination of a teaching that does, indeed, attempt to arbitrarily exclude these texts.

e Matthew 24:36-41 will be discussed further in chapter 13.

regardless of what the ***taken*** of verses 40 and 41 refers to, verse 29 has already established that these events will happen ***Immediately after the tribulation of those days.***[a]

The Church Meets the Lord in the Clouds

1 Thessalonians 4:15-17 - ***[15]****For this we say unto you by the word of the Lord, that we which are alive and remain unto the coming of the Lord shall not prevent them which are asleep.*** ***[16]****For the Lord himself shall descend from heaven with a shout, with the voice of the archangel, and with the trump of God: and the dead in Christ shall rise first:*** ***[17]****Then we which are alive and remain shall be caught up together with them in the clouds, to meet the Lord in the air: and so shall we ever be with the Lord.***

This text is perhaps the most distinct in Scripture specifically dealing with the Rapture of the Church. Though many teach that the Rapture of the Church will happen secretly or silently, these verses speak of a very public and noisy event. The event described here is heralded by a ***shout*** from the Lord, by ***the voice of the archangel, and with the trump of God.*** It appears obvious that Christ Jesus intends His return to be an earth shaking event. When Christ comes for His Church He will come as her triumphal Champion. This triumphal return will not be secretive or silent. The clear statements of the Word of God affirm that His return will be very overt, loud, and jubilant!

Even though some teach that this ***shout*** of the Lord will be a quiet or silent shout, or, more precisely, a shout only heard by believers, it is described in this passage as a distinctly noisy outcry, heard by all the earth's inhabitants. From this text one thing should be perfectly clear to the student of the Word; the triple reference to resounding heralds of Christ's return (the Lord's shout, the archangel's voice, and God's trump) are given to identify this event as a public and obvious event, one that the whole world will be called to witness.

---

a Matthew 24:29.

Note also that this passage looks to be a parallel text to Matthew 24:29-31 and Mark 13:24-27. In all three passages the Lord is pictured as descending to earth in the clouds of heaven. In all three passages Scripture declares that while descending the Lord will call for His Church, or the elect, to meet Him in the air. Also in all three, a distinct and world-wide celestial event takes place. In both the Matthew text and the 1 Thessalonians text the sound of a trumpet precedes the catching up and gathering of the believers in the air. It seems to be without dispute that the Rapture of the Church is the subject of each of these texts. Therefore, if indeed each text is describing the same event, then the Scriptural chronology of the Rapture of the Church is fixed for certain to be ***Immediately after the tribulation of those days.***[a]

Some further things should not be missed in the study of this cardinal Rapture text. First, as was just noted, Christ is not merely hovering in the clouds, He is descending from heaven. At His ascension, angels told the upward gazing disciples that Jesus would come for them ***in like manner as ye have seen him go into heaven.***[b] His ascension was visible and involved Him going from earth to heaven. Therefore, when Christ descends from heaven to receive His disciples, that event must also include His descending all the way to earth, and must also be visible to waiting disciples. Only in this way can the comparative proclamation of the angels (***in like manner***) be fulfilled.

Second, this meeting with the Lord is a specific type of meeting. Including this passage, there are four places in the New Testament where the phrase, ***to meet*** (ἀπάντησις - apontasis), is used. In each case the term refers to a greeting or welcoming. The other three passages are examined below. Notice that each reference connects the phrase, ***to meet***, to a greeting party.

The Christian brethren who lived in Rome came ***to meet*** (greet, welcome) the apostle Paul and the others with him as they journeyed to Rome. These believers greeted Paul and his companions and returned with them to Rome. (***And from thence, when the brethren heard of us,***

---

a Matthew 24:29.

b Acts 1:11.

they came <u>to meet</u> us as far as Appii forum, and The three taverns: whom when Paul saw, he thanked God, and took courage.[a]) Unquestionably the Roman believers who had come out *to meet* the Apostle Paul did not go somewhere else with him after they met him at Appii forum. They went out to welcome him as he approached the city and became part of his escort as he entered the city.

The description of the Rapture in 1 Thessalonians 4 is the same. The believers meet (greet) the Lord in the air as a welcoming party, they then join His escort, and travel back with Him to earth. It seems that the Rapture of the Church will be the divine equivalent of a loving husband embracing his beloved wife as she joyously rushes out to meet him on his return from a long absence. It is at that time that Christ will lovingly summon and receive His Church and continue on with her to earth to set up His millennial kingdom!

The other two times the phrase, *to meet,* is used are found in the parable of the ten virgins. (***Then shall the kingdom of heaven be likened unto ten virgins, which took their lamps, and went forth <u>to meet</u> the bridegroom. And five of them were wise, and five were foolish. They that were foolish took their lamps, and took no oil with them: But the wise took oil in their vessels with their lamps. While the bridegroom tarried, they all slumbered and slept. And at midnight there was a cry made, Behold, the bridegroom cometh; go ye out <u>to meet</u> him. Then all those virgins arose, and trimmed their lamps. And the foolish said unto the wise, Give us of your oil; for our lamps are gone out. But the wise answered, saying, Not so; lest there be not enough for us and you: but go ye rather to them that sell, and buy for yourselves. And while they went to buy, the bridegroom came; and they that were ready went in with him to the marriage: and the door was shut. Afterward came also the other virgins, saying, Lord, Lord, open to us. But he answered and said, Verily I say unto you, I know you not. Watch therefore, for ye know neither the day nor the hour wherein the Son of man cometh.***[b])

---

a Acts 28:15.

b Matthew 25:1-13.

Here again, we see that the meeting described is a welcoming meeting. The ten virgins were already in the bridal chamber. In the wedding custom of the day the bride would expectantly wait for her groom in the bridal chamber, not knowing the exact time or from what direction he would come. A forewarning cry would signal the groom's approach. At that moment the bride would rush out, searching for her groom to welcome him. After greeting him, the two of them would go together into the wedding chamber for the wedding ceremony and marriage banquet. The bridal chamber and the wedding chamber were in the same vicinity, and very often were part of the same building.

The symbolism of the bride rushing out to greet her groom represented that she had forsaken her previous life to cleave unto him. This expectant greeting was a crucial part of the Jewish wedding ceremony. Being unprepared to meet her groom was shameful and communicated two possible attitudes. Either, she did not want to give up all her own life, possessions, and relationships for her groom; or, she was waiting for someone else. Notice that the five foolish virgins knew where the wedding party was (see verse 11,) but since they did not go out to meet their bridegroom they were excluded from entering into the marriage chamber.

This parable of the Ten Virgins may also be a Scriptural analytical story describing an actual future redemptive event. The setting and preparations surrounding the prophesied *marriage supper of the Lamb*[a] are similar to this parable in many particulars. Evidently the Lord Jesus will receive His Church in the Rapture and continue to earth with her where the marriage supper will take place. Revelation 19 describes it quite clearly. In verses 9-11 the bride, who is still on earth, is prepared for the banquet. Verses 11-16 describe the triumphal return of Christ. All this is pictured to be taking place at the end of the time of Great Tribulation and just before the setting up of the millennial kingdom

This parabolic description of what will actually occur on earth when Christ Jesus returns to set up His millennial kingdom includes a very

---

a See Revelation 19.

important directive for the Church. The bride of Christ is admonished to wait with oil in her lamp in a state of continual readiness. When called, she is to expectantly go out to greet her Lord. Participating in this greeting of Christ will attest to the believer's readiness, therefore all spiritual diligence should be given to be present at that reception!

Christ's Coming and the Gathering of the Church

2 Thessalonians 2:1-3 - ¹Now we beseech you, brethren, by the coming of our Lord Jesus Christ, and by our gathering together unto him, ²That ye be not soon shaken in mind, or be troubled, neither by spirit, nor by word, nor by letter as from us, as that the day of Christ is at hand. ³Let no man deceive you by any means: for that day shall not come, except there come a falling away first, and that man of sin be revealed, the son of perdition.

Here the Bible includes both, ***the coming of our Lord Jesus Christ, and ...our gathering together unto him****,* as parts of the same singular event (***that day****,* vs. 3.) Note that the order of Christ's return is ***coming*** first, then ***gathering****.* This is the same order that is seen in the Olivet Discourse.[a] What is also proclaimed here is that two events must occur before the Christians' ***gathering together unto him*** can occur. (1), a great apostasy (***falling away***) from the one true faith will occur, and (2), the Antichrist (***man of sin/son of perdition***) will be revealed. The Apostle Paul admonished the Thessalonian believers not to be deceived by any teachers that taught otherwise (verse 3.) It seems that God's emphatic instruction to His Church is that she is to plan to contend with the Antichrist before expecting her Rapture.

The Falling Away*.* Some teach that the phrase, *falling away,* refers to the Rapture itself, noting that it can also be translated, "departure." However, that understanding is surely not the meaning of this sign. In this text, Paul comforted the Thessalonians by telling them that they

---

a See Matthew 24:30-31 & Mark 13:26-27.

were not to believe that the coming of the Lord and the Rapture (*our gathering*) were ready to take place. Why? Because two necessary precursory events had not yet occurred. It makes no sense to say that the Rapture (*gathering*) cannot happen yet, because the Rapture (*falling away*) must happen before the Rapture (*gathering*) happens. The phrase, *our gathering*, obviously refers to the Rapture of the Church. If *falling away* also refers to the Rapture, then would not Paul be saying to the Thessalonians that the Rapture must precede the Rapture? Nonsensical!

The Greek word used here is apostasy (ἀποστασία - *apostasia*.) It is used two times in the New Testament. Here, rendered, *falling away*, and in Acts 21:21, rendered, *forsake*. The word means, *defection from truth, apostasy, falling away, forsake.*[a] What this text reveals is that before *the coming of our Lord Jesus Christ, and ...our gathering together unto him*, a great *falling away* (apostasy) from the one true faith will occur on earth. This *falling away* is described in many places in the Bible. Some examples include: *Now the Spirit speaketh expressly, that in the latter times some shall depart from the faith, giving heed to seducing spirits, and doctrines of devils;*[b] and, *For the time will come when they will not endure sound doctrine; but after their own lusts shall they heap to themselves teachers, having itching ears; And they shall turn away their ears from the truth, and shall be turned unto fables.*[c] This *falling away*, or apostasy, is a sign that must precede Christ's return and the Rapture of the Church.[d]

The Man of Sin Revealed. Many who hold to pretribulationism say that the Antichrist will not be revealed until after the Church is raptured. According to 2 Thessalonians 2:3 those who believe such teachings have been deceived! The revealing of the *man of sin*, or the *son of perdition* must take place before the Lord returns for His Church. This

---

a James Strong, <u>The Greek Dictionary of the NT</u>, pg. 15, #646.

b 1 Timothy 4:1.

c 2 Timothy 4:3-4.

d This sign will be examined more closely in chapters 23 and 25.

is the unmistakable counsel Paul is giving here. The Thessalonians feared that *the day of Christ* was about to happen (*is at hand.*) This apparently communicated some concern of trouble or woe to them. Paul comforted these believers by explaining that Christ's return was not *at hand.* This is true because *that day (the coming of our Lord Jesus Christ, and... our gathering together unto him*) could not occur until these two signs had come to pass. His statement is very emphatic, *Let no man deceive you by any means: for that day shall not come, except there come a falling away first, and that man of sin be revealed, the son of perdition.*[a]

Do you see the vital significance of this passage in establishing the right timing of the Rapture? This text establishes for certain that the Rapture of the Church (*our gathering together unto him*) will occur at Christ's second coming, and after the great apostasy and the revealing of the Antichrist. These events occur, or come to full realization, during the Tribulation period. Since both events must occur before Christians are gathered unto the Lord, then it is sure that the Rapture (*our gathering*) will take place after the Tribulation.

The great apostasy will likely begin before the Tribulation, but it will not be fully realized until the revealing of the Antichrist. That event will assuredly take place during the Tribulation period. Indeed, the Antichrist will not be fully revealed until he commits *the abomination of desolation.*[b] That desecration is not scheduled to take place until the middle of the seventieth week of Daniel's prophecy (i.e. the middle of the Tribulation.) The following prophecy evidently foretells of the day when both the *falling away* and the revealing of *that man of sin* will be realized: *And I saw one of his heads as it were wounded to death; and his deadly wound was healed: and all the world wondered after the beast. And they worshipped the dragon which gave power unto the beast: and they worshipped the beast, saying, Who is like unto the beast? who is able to make war with*

---

a 2 Thessalonians 2:3.

b Matthew 24:15. See also Daniel 9:27, 12:11.

him?[a] The evil day spoken of here is what the Church of God has been expressly told to prepare for. The definite understanding is that Christ Jesus will not return for the Church until these signs have come to pass.

It seems clear that the central purpose of this 2 Thessalonians text is to strengthen the understanding of Christ's Church by revealing some very specific events that must occur before Christ will return for His bride. These events were signs that the Thessalonians were directed to look for. They were told that these events must come to pass before they were to expect Christ to come for them. These signs clearly establish that the timing of the Rapture of the Church will be after the major events germane to the Great Tribulation have occurred. Since this is Christ's instruction to His Church, why do so few seem to receive it in these last days?

Another issue is raised by this concern, or trouble of spirit, that the Thessalonian Christians had when they thought the Lord's return was **at hand**. Paul wrote to these believers that they should **be not soon shaken in mind, or be troubled, neither by spirit, nor by word, nor by letter as from us, as that the day of Christ is at hand.**[b] Consider this remarkable statement. Have you ever asked yourself why the Thessalonian Christians would **be troubled** about such news? Could this **shaken in mind** refer to their awareness that Great Tribulation will precede **the day of Christ**? Why else might the Thessalonians be troubled about **that day**? There is no rebuke from the apostle in this passage, but assuredly there would have been, if a worldly minded unwillingness for Christ to return was the reason for their concern. The distress addressed here seems to emerged from the knowledge of some woe surrounding **the day of Christ** that made them fearful. Possibly they were afraid that they were running out of time and were not fully prepared for that day or had not yet evangelized their society. This Gentile Church evidently expected great trouble and great tribulation to surround Christ's return for them.

---

a Revelation 13:3-4.

b 2 Thessalonians 2:2.

A further point must not be missed either. Paul's counsel to the Thessalonians specifically directed them to look for the fulfillment of prophetic signs first before expecting the return of Christ and the Rapture of the Church. **They were not told** that the Rapture could happen without warning. Quite the contrary, **they were told** that some very specific events must occur before the Rapture of the Church can occur.[a] This counsel is missing today in many discourses about last things. In some circles, teachers are ridiculed if they advocate that specific signs must be fulfilled before the Rapture can occur. Yet this is clearly the Biblical counsel for the Church of Jesus Christ. Teachers of pretribulationism are often heard saying things like, "*I'm not looking for signs, I'm listening for sounds*" (meaning the sound of the trumpet call.) Nevertheless, it was the distinct directive from the Apostle Paul that Christ's Church should look for specific signs to be fulfilled first, before they were to expect the sounding of the *last trump*.

The Believer's Glorification at the Last Trump

1 Corinthians 15:51-52 - [51]Behold, I shew you a mystery; We shall not all sleep, but we shall all be changed, [52]In a moment, in the twinkling of an eye, at the last trump: for the trumpet shall sound, and the dead shall be raised incorruptible, and we shall be changed. [53]For this corruptible must put on incorruption, and this mortal must put on immortality. [54]So when this corruptible shall have put on incorruption, and this mortal shall have put on immortality, then shall be brought to pass the saying that is written, Death is swallowed up in victory.

This passage will be examined more fully in chapter three, but is included here to demonstrate that the resurrection and Rapture of the saints of God and the glorification of the Church will occur at the time of the trumpet sounding of Christ's return. The text is clear, stating that

---

a This point will be taken up again in chapter 10.

the trumpet shall sound, and the dead shall be raised incorruptible, and we shall be changed.   Since the *first resurrection*[a] (the resurrection of the righteous) happens after the Great Tribulation[b] (for it includes those who were martyred during the Tribulation) and since the apostle Paul established here that this event occurs *at the last trump*, it seems quite clear that the resurrection, Rapture, and glorification of the Church occurs at the very moment of Christ's return.

The designation, *last trump*, is undoubtedly a significant one. It refers not only to the time-order of the trumpet call of the believers' Rapture and glorification, but also to the finality of this redemptive event. I definitely believe that the Holy Spirit used the word *last* because He meant *last*. Could there be any other reason for the identification of the place-order of this trumpet call? Since trumpet blasts are characteristically associated with the events surrounding the Great Tribulation and the coming of Christ, then it follows that when the Bible declares a trumpet blast to be the last one, then there is significance in that designation!

---

a Tribulations saints are distinctly included in the *first resurrection*. See Revelation 20:4-6.

b See chapter 9 for a more thorough examination of the timing of the first resurrection.

2:   A Thief in the Night

The simile of Christ coming as a **thief**[a] (also, **thief in the night**[b]) is used several times in the New Testament as a description of how He will come. Many believe that the Bible teaches that the Lord wants to surprise His Church by coming upon her as **a thief in the night**.[c] They conclude that the **thief** passages declare that the Lord intends to snatch His Church out of the world in a sudden and secretive manner to her, and the rest of the world's, unwitting surprise and amazement. It is important that the student of Scripture examine these texts to understand God's reasons for using this metaphor.

Does the Bible teach that Christ intends to surprise His prepared bride by His return? Absolutely no! In reality the Bible teaches quite the reverse. Christ will only surprise the ungodly and unprepared by His return. To Christians, the Bible emphatically proclaims, **ye brethren are not in darkness, that that day should overtake you as a thief**.[d] The Church of Jesus Christ is definitely not supposed to be surprised by Christ's second coming.

Included below are all seven **thief** references used in the New Testament which refer to the return of Christ. Notice that being caught as if by **a thief** has a bad connotation in each of these seven texts. On examination, these texts teach that it would be devastating for the servant of Lord to be surprised by his Lord's return. No Christ-honoring Christian should desire to be surprised by the Lord as by **a thief in the night**. God has clearly commanded His Church to be watchful and ready so that His coming does not surprise her **as a thief**.

#1: **Matthew 24:42-44 -   [42]Watch therefore: for ye know not what hour your Lord doth come. [43]But know this, that if the goodman**

---

a See Matthew 24:43, Luke 12:39, 1 Thessalonians 5:4, & Revelation 3:3, 16:15.

b See 1 Thessalonians 5:2 & 2 Peter 3:10.

c Some readers may remember that a popular Christian movie of the early 1970's, promoting the pretribulation Rapture scenario, was entitled, "A Thief in the Night."

d 1 Thessalonians 5:4.

of the house had known in what watch the <u>thief</u> would come, he would have watched, and would not have suffered his house to be broken up. ⁴⁴Therefore be ye also ready: for in such an hour as ye think not the Son of man cometh.

#2: *Luke 12:37-40 - ³⁷Blessed are those servants, whom the lord when he cometh shall find watching: verily I say unto you, that he shall gird himself, and make them to sit down to meat, and will come forth and serve them. ³⁸And if he shall come in the second watch, or come in the third watch, and find them so, blessed are those servants. ³⁹And this know, that <u>if the goodman of the house had known what hour the <u>thief</u> would come, he would have watched, and not have suffered his house to be broken through.</u> ⁴⁰Be ye therefore ready also: for the Son of man cometh at an hour when ye think not.*

The clear proclamation of these first two texts is that it would be an awful thing for Christ's return to surprise a believer like *a thief*. The Lord strenuously admonished His servants to give their fullest effort so that they will not be caught off guard by His return. The diligent Christian is he who watches, and is therefore cognizant of and prepared for Christ's coming. In the Luke reference Jesus exhorts His servants to be alert and at watch at all times. He proclaimed that even if He comes at the second or third watch of the night they should be alert and in expectation of Him. It is the *goodman of the house* who watches and is therefore not caught off guard by the Lord's return.

#'s 3 & 4: *1 Thessalonians 5:1-6 - ¹But of the times and the seasons, brethren, ye have no need that I write unto you. ²For yourselves know perfectly that <u>the day of the Lord so cometh as a <u>thief in the night</u>. ³For when they shall say, Peace and safety; then sudden destruction cometh upon them, as travail upon a woman with child; and they shall not escape. ⁴<u>But ye, brethren, are not in darkness, that that day should overtake you as a <u>thief</u>.</u> ⁵Ye are all the children of light, and the children of the day: we are not of the* *night, nor of darkness. ⁶Therefore let us not sleep, as do others;* *but <u>let us watch and be sober.</u>*

This text records the third and fourth uses of the ***thief*** metaphor. Let it first be emphatically noted that there must be something to watch for if the Church is commanded to ***watch!*** By charging the church with these words, ***Therefore let us not sleep, as do others; but let us watch and be sober***, the Apostle Paul is expressly declaring that there will be indicators of Christ's return which the Church should be watching for.

These verses manifestly declare who will and who will not be surprised by Christ's return. Verse four makes it quite clear that **believers are not supposed to be surprised by Christ's return**. Verse two verifies that Christ will surprise the ungodly with sudden destruction by coming to the world as ***a thief in the night***. Notice the Apostle's distinction here. When speaking of the wicked, he used third-person pronouns and stated, ***For when <u>they</u> shall say...*** and ***sudden destruction cometh upon <u>them</u>...*** But when speaking of the believers he used a second-person pronoun and stated, ***But <u>ye</u>, brethren...*** It is quite clear in this text who will be surprised by the Lord's return, and who must not be surprised by His return.

Verses four through six verify that the righteous are not to be taken by surprise by the coming of the Lord Jesus Christ. The text is very clear, stating, ***But ye, brethren, are not in darkness, that that day should overtake you as a thief.***[a] Therefore, it is Scripturally unsound to teach that Jesus intends to surprise the Church by His coming. In reality the opposite is the Scriptural truth. Christ does **NOT** intend to surprise Christians by His coming. He even earnestly pleads with His Church to be watchful and prepared so that she will not be surprised.

It is undoubtedly true that the main focus of the preparedness called for in these ***thief*** texts is the spiritual preparedness that comes from being *"washed in the blood of the Lamb."* Some may note that the emphasis is on spiritual preparedness for His coming not on intellectual

---

a 1 Thessalonians 5:4.

knowledge of His coming. This is certainly true. However, these texts also make it expressly clear that no Christian should be surprised by Christ's return. Regardless of what the main focus of the preparedness called for here is, believers are responsible to be engaged in it and they have no excuse for being surprised by Christ's return. Therefore, it is not proper to teach that God is planning to surprise His Church by His glorious return. God's word declares just the opposite and any teaching that advances an unexpected coming is liable to distract or mislead believers. Remember this distinct admonition, *ye, brethren, are not in darkness, that that day should overtake you as a thief!*[a]

#5: *2 Peter 3:10 - But <u>the day of the Lord will come as a thief in the night</u>; in the which the heavens shall pass away with a great noise, and the elements shall melt with fervent heat, the earth also and the works that are therein shall be burned up.*

    This fifth passage foretells of the destruction by fire of all creation affected by the fall. The focus is on the final conflagration that will occur at the end of the Lord's millennial reign. The focus of the *day of the Lord* described here is on the full scope of Christ's redemption and the cleansing of His sin-corrupted creation. Yet, again, the sense of *thief* is negative. In Scripture when *thief* is used in reference to Christ's coming it always bodes of punishment or wrath. It is absolutely not a metaphor to describe how Christ's Church will be affected by His coming! The Church is continually warned to be prepared so she will not be surprised by His return as if by *a thief in the night*.

#6: *Revelation 3:3 - Remember therefore how thou hast received and heard, and hold fast, and repent. If therefore thou shalt not watch, I will come on thee as a <u>thief</u>, and thou shalt not know what hour I will come upon thee.*

---

a 1 Thessalonians 5:4.

Again, the clarity of meaning of the usage of *thief* here cannot be mistaken. From this sixth passage we see that the Lord is using the *thief* simile as a warning and reprimand. Only the heedless and negligent will have the Lord come upon them *as a thief.* The Lord directly warned the Sardis Christians here that their negligence and indifference would result in disaster! What would that disaster be? The disaster would be Christ coming upon them *as a thief* because of their culpable ignorance of the hour of His coming. Being surprised as by *a thief* is clearly a judgment. It defines how the unprepared will experience His return! It does not describe Christ's prepared bride's experience!

Hence, Christians better not expect to be shocked by Christ's return as if by a *thief in the night.* That would be disastrous! These *thief* passages conclusively reveal that Christ Jesus has commanded His Church to be prepared so that she will not be caught off guard and surprised as if by *a thief.*

#7: *Revelation 16:15 - Behold, <u>I come as a thief.</u> Blessed is he that watcheth, and keepeth his garments, lest he walk naked, and they see his shame.*

This seventh, and last, reference is found in a passage describing the latter part of the Tribulation period. In this text Christ warns faithful believers in the midst of the Tribulation to be watchful so His coming to the world *as a thief* will not surprise them or catch them off guard. It is interesting to note that in this context mankind has already endured most of the Tribulation period, yet Christ is still warning His Church that He will *come as a thief* upon the unprepared. Note that even Great Tribulation believers are prophetically warned to be watchful so they are not surprised by His coming.

Many who hold to a pretribulation Rapture viewpoint maintain that the posttribulational viewpoint destroys any surprise element of the Rapture. The argument is that once the Tribulation period begins then it would be a simple matter of counting the days. But the believers in view in Revelation 16:15 are far into the Tribulation period and there is still an uncertainty as to when Christ will come. Notice that this is an admonition given to the believers on earth during the time of the sixth angel's outpoured vial of wrath. The believers in view here are alive during the latter part of the Great Tribulation and are still commanded to watch lest they be found unprepared.

In conclusion, surely it is manifestly evident that the ***thief*** simile refers to the demise of the wicked at the return of Christ. ***Thief*** does not refer to the Rapture of the Church. These references describe the shock due to unpreparedness that the world will experience at Christ's return. This is Scripturally put in clear distinction to the God-directed readiness of the Bride of Christ. Therefore, since this metaphor describes the trauma, horror, and destruction that will engulf the ungodly and unprepared when the Lord returns for His bride, and since the faithful and prepared Church is waiting in discerning expectation for her Bridegroom, no God-fearing Christian should desire to be surprised by Christ's coming. Rather, he should be watchfully prepared with the definite Biblical admonition before him that he not be surprised by the Lord's return as if by ***a thief in the night***.

3:   In the Twinkling of an Eye

*1 Corinthians 15:51-54 - *[51]*Behold, I shew you a mystery; We shall not all sleep, but we shall all be changed, *[52]*In a moment, in the twinkling of an eye, at the last trump: for the trumpet shall sound, and the dead shall be raised incorruptible, and we shall be changed. *[53]*For this corruptible must put on incorruption, and this mortal must put on immortality. *[54]*So when this corruptible shall have put on incorruption, and this mortal shall have put on immortality, then shall be brought to pass the saying that is written, Death is swallowed up in victory.*

Many have mistakenly taught that this text states that Christ's coming for the Church will happen *In a moment, in the twinkling of an eye*. Pretribulationists typically differentiate this supposed sudden and momentary coming of Christ from His actual return to earth to set up His millennial kingdom. But, upon examination, we quickly see that the, *in the twinkling of an eye*, statement is not describing Christ's return. The phrase proclaims that the believer's *change* will happen *in the twinkling of an eye,* not the return of Christ. The antecedent phrase of the phrase, *In a moment, in the twinkling of an eye*, is, *we shall all be changed*. It is not the Lord's return, but the glorification *change* to be affected upon the living and resurrected saints that will take place *In a moment, in the twinkling of an eye*.

It is vitally important that the reader understand this distinction. There is a great deal of folklore in the modern Church about a sudden and unexplained world-wide disappearance of Christians.[a] Many use this very text as a proof of this assumption. This text, however, does not justify any such teaching. We can positively affirm here that the glorification of the believers will be instantaneous, but we must not assume that the second coming of Christ will be. This passage does not even specifically mention the return of Christ. The focus of this passage

---

[a] This subject will be taken up further in chapter 13.

is upon the fact of the resurrection. In this chapter the Apostle Paul refutes a devastating heresy which denied that there will be a resurrection of the believers who have died in the Lord.

The Bible plainly verifies here that indeed there will be a glorious resurrection of the redeemed and that both the living and resurrected saints will then be instantaneously glorified, hallelujah! By cross referencing we know that this resurrection and instantaneous glorification will occur at the second coming of Christ and the Rapture of the Church. This text, however, is primarily directed at the reality, purpose, and wonder of the resurrection. The focus is on the glorious and complete redemption which will be realized by all believers on that resurrection morning.

The following reference also alludes to this sudden transformation of the redeemed and does expressly place the timing of this glorious transformation to be at the very return of Christ: *Beloved, now are we the sons of God, and it doth not yet appear what we shall be: but we know that, when he shall appear, we shall be like him; for we shall see him as he is.*[a] It is when the Lord Jesus Christ actually comes for His bride that the long-awaited glorification of the saints will occur. There is a cause and effect sequence here. We will be *like him* because *we shall see him as he is*.

Yet, neither of these passages allow for an understanding that the Lord's return will be momentary. There is a sense of finality here that alludes to the settling of accounts and consummation of all things. This concluding and judgment is scheduled to occur at the physical return of Christ to set up His millennial kingdom. This, we know, will take place *Immediately after the tribulation of those days*.[b]

Please notice, also, that this 1 Corinthians 15 text gives another very important clue as to the timing of the Rapture. According to this passage the glorification and Rapture of the Church will occur *at the last trump*. In Revelation there are several references to trumpets being sounded during the Tribulation period. Especially the *seven trumpet*

a 1 John 3:2

b Matthew 24:29

judgments recorded in Revelation chapters 9-11. For this to actually be the *last trump*, as the text plainly states, it must be the last one recorded, or occur after those Great Tribulation trumpet blasts.

The Biblical description given before the seventh angel sounds his trumpet is quite interesting: ***But in the days of the voice of the seventh angel, when he shall begin to sound, the mystery of God should be finished, as he hath declared to his servants the prophets.***[a] This reference discloses that the seventh trumpet blast will include more than judgment. In it also *the mystery of God* will be finished. Mystery,[b] in the New Testament, most often refers to the whole or some part of God's redemption plan. So it seems that this seventh trumpet blast will also signal some final act of redemption. Could this final act of redemption be the *mystery* that the Apostle Paul pointed to when he wrote, ***Behold, I shew you a mystery***? Is it the Rapture and glorification of the Church of God?

Of course, 1 Corinthians 15:51 does not state that the *last trump* is the seventh trumpet blast of Revelation, but it is clear that it is either that seventh blast or one occurring after that blast. The term *last trump* is definitive! Bible student, could *last* mean anything other than *last?* As was noted earlier, would the Holy Spirit use *last trump* if He meant anything other than *last trump?*

The prophetic texts of Scripture do not record any reference to the sounding of trumpets after the immediate period surrounding the Great Tribulation. The *last trump* referenced here is assuredly the same *great sound of a trumpet,*[c] recorded in the Olivet Discourse. When that trumpet sounds the angels will go forth to gather Christ's *elect from the four winds, from one end of heaven to the other.*[d] We have the clear statement of Scripture affirming that that trumpet call will sound ***Immediately after the tribulation of those days.***[e]

---

a Revelation 10:7.

b See chapter 14 for an in-depth examination of the meaning of "*mystery doctrines.*"

c Matthew 24:31.

d Ibid.

e Matthew 24:29.

In summary, some very important truths surrounding the return of Christ are illuminated by this passage. Both the redemptive events accompanying the Rapture and the timing of the Rapture are clarified. This **resurrection** and **change** of the saints of God is the culminating event of redemption. Since the Bible distinctly proclaims that the **first resurrection**[a] will occur after the Great Tribulation, and since it is also plainly established in Scripture that the Rapture includes the resurrection of the righteous, then the timing of the Rapture is established. It will occur at the return of Christ and after the Great Tribulation.

There are some further eschatological discoveries here. We find that it is at the moment of the Rapture that both the resurrected and living saints of God will be instantaneously glorified. Those who have died in Christ are with Him in spirit, but will not receive their glorified bodies until the Rapture. Also we discover the notable truth that this resurrection and glorification of the saints will occur at the **last trump**. And since we know that a trumpet blast will herald Christ's return, and since we know that the resurrection and glorification of the saints will take place when Christ actually appears[b] in the clouds, then we also can be sure that the resurrection, glorification, and Rapture of the saints will occur **Immediately after the tribulation of those days.**[c]

---

a See Revelation 20:4-6. See chapter 9 for an in depth study of the timing of the *First Resurrection*.

b See Colossians 3:4. The distinct meaning of *appear* will be examined in chapter 15.

c Matthew 24:29.

4:   Looking for an Escape

In His high-priestly prayer, the Lord Jesus prayed, *I pray not that thou shouldest take them out of the world, but that thou shouldest keep them from the evil.*[a]   Indeed, Jesus proclaimed to His followers that *In the world ye shall have tribulation: but be of good cheer; I have overcome the world.*[b]   The Scripture even exhorts the Church to *glory in tribulations also: knowing that tribulation worketh patience.*[c]

An incident of persecution that the Apostle Paul endured is particularly instructive to the living Church of the last days. After being stoned and left for dead, the Bible proclaims the wonderful truth that the Apostle Paul rose up and went to Derbe. There, he preached a mighty sermon and then exhorted the believers: *Confirming the souls of the disciples, and exhorting them to continue in the faith, and that we must through much tribulation enter into the kingdom of God.*[d]   What a clear and definitive statement!   This counsel is the consistent instruction that God gives to His Church.

Yet, many Christians believe that the Lord plans to take His Church out of the world before the coming Great Tribulation. This belief does not seem to be compatible with God's intentions for His Church. Jesus told His disciples that He sent them into the world as *lambs among wolves.*   Christ's command to His disciples was, *Go your ways: behold, I send you forth as lambs among wolves.*[e]   But Christian, you serve the God *that is able to keep you from falling, and to present you faultless before the presence of his glory with exceeding joy.*[f]   He has sent believers forth as His ambassadors. In this commission, Christ has not promised His disciples a life free of tribulation and persecution.   He

---

a John 17:15.

b John 16:33.

c Romans 5:3.

d Acts 14:22.

e Luke 10:3.

f Jude 1:24.

does, however, speak this promise concerning the child of His love, *I will be with him in trouble; I will deliver him, and honour him.*[a]

There is a seeming incongruity with God's purposes for His Church and this pretribulation escape doctrine. To believe in a physical removal of the Church from earth, or escape out of this world's trouble, is also to believe that Christ will pull His witness to fallen men out of the world in mankind's greatest hour of need. God has not directed His faithful children to seek escape. Rather, He has directed them to pray for boldness. (*And now, Lord, behold their threatenings: and grant unto thy servants, that with all boldness they may speak thy word.*[b])

Since this belief in an escape out of the Tribulation at least looks like a teaching that is not consistent with the Church's great commission, an examination of some passages were pretribulationists believe God has promised just such an escape, is in order.

Luke 21:34-36 - *[34]And take heed to yourselves, lest at any time your hearts be overcharged with surfeiting, and drunkenness, and cares of this life, and so that day come upon you unawares. [35]For as a snare shall it come on all them that dwell on the face of the whole earth. [36]<u>Watch ye therefore, and pray always, that ye may be accounted worthy to escape all these things that shall come to pass, and to stand before the Son of man.</u>*

Verse 36 of this passage is seen by some as an "escape by Rapture" text. However, there are some key factors about this text that point to a much different type of *escape*. Verse 34 here is another example of the many texts in Scripture calling the faithful to be watchful and circumspect lest *that day come upon you unawares*. The escape that the Lord promised in verse 36 is an escape related to the preparedness and watchfulness He called for in verse 34. Christ warned His followers about backsliding into sin and excess. Indeed, He has warned

a Psalm 91:15.

b Acts 4:29.

His Church that a ***snare*** of destruction will come upon the ungodly and the heedless. Believers are admonished to ***take heed***, lest that same ***snare*** take them as well. The ***escape*** mentioned here is an escape out of the destruction and damnation that the wicked will be subjected to. It is the blessing of being ushered into the very presence of the Lord.

Jesus made it quite clear in this context that the very followers to which He promised this deliverance will be present on earth during ***these things that shall come to pass***. For this reason, He warned of their need to watch against sin. If they watch they will escape damnation and stand before Him when he comes to separate the wicked and righteous ***one from another, as a shepherd divideth his sheep from the goats.***[a] It is clear that the ***escape*** spoken of in this passage is an escape from damnation. It is a Christ-afforded worthiness to ***stand before the Son of man***.

Another fact should not be overlooked. This text is part of the Olivet Discourse, which those who believe in a pretribulation Rapture typically claim does not apply to the Church.[b] It seems a strained interpretation to pull this verse out of a context that is supposedly "inapplicable" to the Church and use it as a proof-text for a Rapture escape for the Church. The righteous whom Jesus is speaking of here are conclusively seen to be present on earth during the time of trouble.[c] Hence, this watchful escape is not referencing a physical removal, it is referencing an overcoming victory over sin and the world.

Revelation 3:10 - Because thou hast kept the word of my patience, <u>I also will keep thee from the hour of temptation, which shall come upon all the world</u>, to try them that dwell upon the earth.

This verse is assuredly the pretribulationist's favorite "escape by Rapture" text. Yet again, the context here lends to a much different

---

a Matthew 25:32.

b Discussed further in chapters 11 & 12.

c See Luke 21:8, 12-20, 34-35.

interpretation. To the faithful Church at Philadelphia, Christ Jesus made the following promise, *I also will keep thee from the hour of temptation, which shall come upon all the world.*[a] This promise is given to a literal first century Church that had proven herself faithful to Christ. This faithfulness is set in contrast to most of the other six Churches receiving letters in Revelation. Therefore, this promise is the distinct reward to the Church in Philadelphia. A reward which that congregation received when other congregations were rebuked.

Since this is clearly a particular reward to first century Philadelphian believers, then the first fulfilment of this pledge must have been for that literal congregation. Those blessed brethren at Philadelphia had patiently endured previous tribulation, so the Lord Jesus promised them a special deliverance from the coming world-wide *hour of temptation.* Assuredly this was a reward that those particular, first century believers were to receive. If they did not receive this deliverance personally then would this not have been an empty promise? The first world-wide wave of Roman persecution against the Church happened near the end of the first century. It is likely that whatever this promise refers to, it must have been at least initially realized by those Philadelphian believers and around the time of John's letter.

Understand that these letters were sent to actual Christian churches. For example, the church in Pergamos literally witnessed the martyrdom of Antipas, and had members of the Nicolaitan cult[b] among its ranks. The warnings and rewards mentioned in Revelation chapters two and three were initially for those original seven Asia Minor congregations.

We must apply this message to a real first century Church before we can apply it to the last days Church. It is not likely that this promise meant that Christ was going to physically remove the first century Philadelphian Church from the earth. Therefore, it need not mean that He will physically remove the "last days" Church from the earth either. Both pretribulationists and posttribulationists, typically reject the idea

---

a Revelation 3:10

b See Revelation 2:13-15.

of a "partial Rapture" of only a faithful part or faithful parts of the Church. At best, this verse could promise a "Rapture escape" for only one-seventh of these Asian Churches. The Lord's, *I... will keep thee from the hour of temptation,*[a] promise is specifically individualized to the Philadelphian believers and clearly meant that the Lord would distinctly protect those faithful believers.

Since this commendation of Christ is included in Holy Writ it has a relevance for the whole Church of Jesus Christ throughout the ages, but the application of this promise to subsequent Christian generations, and to the "last days" Church, must be consistent with its first meaning. Is it believed that Christ physically removed these first century believers from the earth? If the answer to that question is no, then there is no need to believe that this verse necessitates a physical removal from earth to any other group or age of Christian believers.

As to the end times application of this promise, indeed, the Great Tribulation seems to be prophetically foreshadowed here. Nevertheless, since the first century and primary application of this promise did not result in a removal of that Church from the earth, then the "last days" application need not either. In his book, <u>Contemporary Options in Eschatology</u>, Millard J. Erickson gives sound end-times understanding to the meaning of the promise to *I... will keep thee from the hour of temptation.*

> *Revelation 3:10 - 'Because thou hast kept the word of my patience, I also will keep (τηρέω) thee from (ἐκ) the hour of temptation, which shall come upon all the world, to try them that dwell upon the earth.' The interpretation of this verse turns on the significance of the preposition ἐκ. ...[T]he primary sense of ἐκ, 'emergence from within,' refutes the pretribulational interpretation of the verse. For the church to emerge from within the hour of testing, it must have been present in that testing.*

---

a Revelation 3:10

It is true that ἐκ and ἀπό ('away from') often denote the same relationship. In those cases, however, it is not because ἐκ has lost the idea of 'out from within' but because ἀπό has added to its central meaning an additional one.

John uses ἐκ approximately 336 times, far more often than any other New Testament writer. In every case the idea of emergence or origin is the meaning most suitable to the context. The Johannine usage of the word, then, appears to be well established.

Pretribulationists sometimes object that if the posttribulational view is correct, then in place of ἐκ would be either διά ('through,') or ἐν ('in'). ...[I]t is a matter of emphasis. Ἐν would have placed all the emphasis on presence within. Διά would have emphasized entrance, presence within, and emergency. But ἐκ puts all the emphasis upon emergence, thus highlighting the final, victorious outcome of the keeping and guarding. The same emphasis appears in Revelation 7:14, where the saints 'came out of (ἐκ) great tribulation.'

The final issue of Revelation 3:10 is the meaning of the verb τηρέω. When a situation of danger is in view, τηρέω means 'guard.' Danger is implicit in the idea of guarding. If the church is in heaven at this time, however, as pretribulationism teaches, then what can be the danger that requires God's protecting hand upon her? Throughout the Septuagint and the New Testament, τηρέω always denotes protection within the sphere of danger.[a]

In his textual analysis of Revelation 3:10, Dr. Erickson has argued quite persuasively against seeing this text as a promise of physical escape from the earth during this time of trouble. Since an analysis of the texts in question do not support the Church's physical removal from earth, and since the general instructions and purpose of the Church

---

a Millard J. Erickson, <u>Contemporary Options in Eschatology</u>, pgs. 154-155.

(being salt and light in the world) do not support such a removal, it seems that Christians would do better to plan, by God's grace, to stand in that dark hour. We should not anticipate an escape by removal, but we should anticipate and look for an escape by overcoming grace! Remember, where sin (evil) abounds, there does grace that much more abound!*[a]*

This Philadelphian congregation had been, by God's grace, faithful to Christ during prior tribulation. Jesus assured them that He would supply this same grace to keep them from succumbing in the coming *hour of temptation* as well. To the Tribulation saints the Lord makes the same promise. He will keep them from temptation, He will deliver them from evil. But this deliverance will not be by physically removing them from the evil. It will be by providentially keeping them from the evil. This understanding is also the only one that is consistent with a promise initially given to the first century Philadelphian Church. That is, of course, unless there was a first century Rapture of that Church.

One final passage will be examined here which some believe contains a promise of an out-of-this-world escape:

2 Thessalonians 1:3-10 - [3]We are bound to thank God always for you, brethren, as it is meet, because that your faith groweth exceedingly, and the charity of every one of you all toward each other aboundeth; [4]So that we ourselves glory in you in the churches of God for your patience and faith in all your persecutions and tribulations that ye endure:

[5]Which is a manifest token of the righteous judgment of God, that ye may be counted worthy of the kingdom of God, for which ye also suffer: [6]<u>Seeing it is a righteous thing with God to recompense tribulation to them that trouble you; [7]And to you who are troubled rest with us, when the Lord Jesus shall be revealed from heaven with his mighty angels,</u> [8]In flaming fire taking vengeance on them that know not God, and that obey not the

---

a See Romans 5:20.

gospel of our Lord Jesus Christ: ⁹*Who shall be punished with everlasting destruction from the presence of the Lord, and from the glory of his power;* ¹⁰*When he shall come to be glorified in his saints, and to be admired in all them that believe (because our testimony among you was believed) in that day.*

It is truly surprising that some have seen in this text a promise to the Church of a physical escape out of the Great Tribulation. Indeed, as a posttribulationist, I would point to this reference as yet another clear passage describing the return of Christ in a posttribulation context. Yet, some have seen a cryptic escape promise here. Verses six and seven have been seen to contain a somewhat hidden promise of Rapture escape to the Church.

Paul stated, *Seeing it is a righteous thing with God to recompense tribulation to them that trouble you; And to you who are troubled rest with us, when the Lord Jesus shall be revealed from heaven with his mighty angels.*[a] Some pretribulationists have noted that this passage expressly states that a righteous act of God will be to visit *tribulation* on the wicked persecutors of Christians, while at the same time granting His faithful Church, *rest*. They note that, indeed, according to their theological viewpoint, the Church will be in heaven enjoying the *rest* and bliss of glory while wicked men go through the *tribulation.*

Again, however, the context here argues against this interpretation. As just noted, this passage is seen by posttribulationists as a clear text that describes the trouble that the Church has and will continue to endure in this world until the return of Christ. The *tribulation* visited on the wicked referenced here is the destruction of the wrath of God. The passage clearly defines how this *tribulation* will come: *In flaming fire taking vengeance on them that know not God, and that obey not the gospel of our Lord Jesus Christ.*[b] The Bible makes it clear that this *tribulation* is the wrath of hell that is coming on the wicked; for the text clearly states that the wicked *shall be punished with everlasting*

---

a 2 Thessalonians 1:6-7.

b 2 Thessalonians 1:8.

destruction from the presence of the Lord, and from the glory of his power.[a]

Also, the timing of the judgment and deliverance spoken of here is expressly established to be when Christ ***shall come to be glorified in his saints, and to be admired in all them that believe.***[b] This is very similar to the context of Matthew 25:31-46 where Christ divides the wicked and the righteous ***When the Son of man shall come in his glory, and all the holy angels with him.***[c]

This is yet another text of Scripture that outlines a clear posttribulation Rapture time-line. The Church is pictured here as facing ***persecutions and tribulations***[d] and then being gloriously delivered by the Lord when He comes with His angels to set up His kingdom. At that coming the wicked are visited with wrath.[e] This, indeed, is the particular doctrine and hope of posttribulationists!!!

What must be understood here is that the two basic viewpoints on the timing of the Rapture are at odds on a crucial point. One promotes the idea that a surprise return of Christ to Rapture the Church out of the earth is the imperative which will compel believers to be ready at all times. This viewpoint requires that the surprise element of the Rapture be kept intact, and tantalizes a ready Church with the promise of escape.

The other viewpoint promotes the idea that the knowledge of coming deception, persecution, and hardship is the imperative that is to compel a continuing state of readiness in Christ's bride. This viewpoint declares that there is no promise of a removal, but there is a promise of sustaining and overcoming grace. What the student of Scripture must spiritually discern is which viewpoint promotes the imperative that the prophetic texts of Scripture call believers to.

---

a 2 Thessalonians 1:9.

b 2 Thessalonians 1:10.

c Matthew 25:31.

d 2 Thessalonians 1:4.

e See chapter 6 for a study of when the wrath of God will be visited upon the wicked.

It is often argued by pretribulationists that their understanding of a Rapture escape is a sobering, fearful truth that will compel believers to be always ready to meet their Lord. Indeed, I have been personally criticized for espousing a belief that supposedly removes this fearful admonition from Christ's Church. However, it is obvious that most, if not all pretribulationists, distinctly prefer their viewpoint as being less difficult than the posttribulationist's alternate view. Though, undoubtedly, pretribulationists believe that their view is the Biblically declared true view, they also believe it to be the easier scenario, humanly speaking. When candid about their true feelings, many pretribulationists would admit that their preference for a Rapture escape is based, at least in part, on the fact that it is more preferable than a belief that bodes of precursory trials and tribulations.[a]

Therefore, if the pretribulation Rapture doctrine is the preferable doctrine because it is an easier way, than it cannot also be the way that compels the most intense preparation. I believe that the pretribulation Rapture viewpoint which offers an escape out of earth is more likely to engender a condition of laxness than it is a state of preparedness. There is an altogether understandable human desire to avoid these end times troubles that are prophesied to come upon the earth. However, this perfectly innocent inclination must never be allowed to cause God's children to reject Biblical truth. Though humanly preferable, a promise of being removed from the sphere of the troubles of the last days seems to be unsupported by Scripture.

The early Christians demonstrated an inspiring attitude when faced with persecution, they prayed not for escape but for boldness to preach the gospel. (***Lord, behold their threatenings: and grant unto thy servants, that with all boldness they may speak thy word.***[b]) May God grant His last-days Church a similar fortitude; May her prayers be for boldness in persecution, not escape from persecution.

---

a Incidentally, I would also prefer a pretribulation Rapture escape if I had the option to choose.

b Acts 4:29.

5:   Will There Be Two Second Comings of Christ?

It was difficult to know just where to place this chapter in this volume. It may be, by some estimations, properly placed first, for there is a great nagging question surrounding the whole pretribulation Rapture perspective.

That question? *How does one avoid the Scripturally unsupportable conclusion that pretribulationism of necessity creates two second comings of Christ?* Pretribulationists assert that the first-second coming of Christ *in the clouds*^{a} will be to Rapture His Church out of the earth. Then, at least seven years later, the second-second coming of Christ *in the clouds*^{b} will occur. The purpose of this coming will be to judge the wicked and set up Christ's millennial kingdom.

Admittedly, they would not describe their view quite that way. Yet, simply put, that accurately expresses the pretribulationist's teaching. Nevertheless, any examination of the Biblical texts that foretell of the glorious second coming of Christ will quickly reveal that there is no such double return to be found!

This twofold return is expressed in many different ways by pretribulationists. Some common descriptions are as follows: *"Christ must come back for the Church before He can come back with the Church."* Also, *"At the Rapture, Christ comes for His Church to receive her unto Himself, at His return, He comes with His Church to set up His millennial kingdom."* And, *"The Rapture is when the Church goes up to heaven, the return is when Christ comes down to earth."*

Yet, in studying the numerous Scriptural passages that refer to the second coming of Christ, it is very clear that the receiving of the Church and the judgment of the wicked will both occur at the same time and are parts of the same event. The Word of God declares that both the reward of the righteous and the judgment of the wicked will occur at the coming of Christ. The clear fact remains that the Bible in no place proclaims that this singular coming will actually be two comings.

---

a See 1 Thessalonians 4:17.

b See Matthew 24:30.

There are over fifty references in the New Testament that use the words, *coming, cometh*, or *shall come*, to describe Christ's second advent. In none of these fifty-plus references does the Scripture describe this event as being actually two events.

In these numerous passages God's Word declares that two momentous things will occur: The wicked will reap destruction (*And then shall that Wicked be revealed, whom the Lord shall consume with the spirit of his mouth, and <u>shall destroy with the brightness of his coming,</u>*[a]) and the righteous will reap the blessed rewards of redemption (*...<u>waiting for the coming of our Lord Jesus Christ: Who shall also confirm you unto the end, that ye may be blameless in the day of our Lord Jesus Christ.</u>*[b])

It is Scripturally untenable to maintain that Christ is actually going to come again two times. A significant number of the fifty-plus references of Christ's coming describe the destruction of the wicked. An equally significant number of these passages forecast the reward of the righteous. And, doubtlessly a surprising discovery to some, many of these passages foretell both proceedings. We might say that one of the surest things that Scripture reveals about the second coming of Christ is that both the wicked and the righteous will have business before the Lord on that day.

Matthew 25:31-34, 41 - [31] When the Son of man shall come in his glory, and all the holy angels with him, then shall he sit upon the throne of his glory: [32] And before him shall be gathered all nations: and he shall separate them one from another, as a shepherd divideth his sheep from the goats: [33] And he shall set the sheep on his right hand, but the goats on the left. [34] Then shall the King say unto them on his right hand, Come, ye blessed of my Father, inherit the kingdom prepared for you from the foundation of the world: ...[41] Then shall he say also unto them on the left

---

a 2 Thessalonians 2:8.

b 1 Corinthians 1:7-8.

hand, Depart from me, ye cursed, into everlasting fire, prepared
for the devil and his angels:

It is hard to imagine a more detailed and precise description of the happenings which will take place when **the Son of man shall come in his glory.** Notice that the Lord stated quite clearly that the separating of the righteous (**the sheep**) from the wicked (**the goats**) will not happen until He has **come in his glory.** The expressed message of this text establishes Christ's second coming as a singular event on a particular day. On this day two distinct events will take place, the righteous will be received into the kingdom of heaven and the wicked will be condemned to **everlasting fire.**

This same pattern is seen in many other texts. Another example is the parable of the Wheat and the Tares. (**Let both grow together until the harvest: and in the time of harvest I will say to the reapers, Gather ye together first the tares, and bind them in bundles to burn them: but gather the wheat into my barn.**[a]) In this parable Jesus expressly proclaimed that first the **tares** will be gathered and bundled for the fire and then the **wheat** will be gathered into His barn. This pattern is the consistent revelation of God's Word. The idea of gathering the Church several years before the judgment of the unrepentant is simply not found in Holy Writ.

In a discussion with one proponent of pretribulationism, I was told that the double return of Christ is foreshadowed by the fact that the Old Testament saints did not know that there would be a first coming and a second coming of Messiah either. Albeit a creative argument, this comparison is hardly appropriate to a Scriptural examination of Christ's second coming. It may very well be true that many Old Testament saints did not understand the gospel plan. They certainly could have missed the fact that in order for man to be redeemed, the Messiah would first have to come as a suffering Servant-Savior before He could come

---

a Matthew 13:30.

as a conquering King-Savior. However, the Old Testament declares that very thing! Isaiah 53 is perhaps the clearest reference in the whole of Scripture*[a]* of the atoning work of ***the Lamb of God, which taketh away the sin of the world.**[b]* It is one thing to say that the Old Testament saints missed this distinction; it is another thing altogether to say that this distinction was not given in the Old Testament.

Remember the discussion that Jesus had with the two disciples on the road to Emmaus? In His conversation He revealed that this great redemption plan had been revealed in the Scriptures (specifically the Old Testament Scriptures), and further, that they were fools for not seeing it. (***Then he said unto them, O fools, and slow of heart to believe all that the prophets have spoken: Ought not Christ to have suffered these things, and to enter into his glory? And beginning at Moses and all the prophets, he expounded unto them in all the scriptures the things concerning himself.**[c]*) The problem with this dual return teaching is that it is simply not found in Scripture.

There is another issue that has arisen from this teaching of a twofold second coming which should be examined. The separation of the second coming into two second comings has apparently left some (or many) unsaved persons with a false sense of security. Namely, they believe that they will have another chance to consider the claims of Christ after the truths of Christ's gospel are proven to them by this disappearance of the Church. These same individuals presently reject the salvation call of Christ.

I have encountered this misguided confidence on several occasions. In witnessing to one man of his need for salvation, I was dumbfounded by the following response. The individual stated, *"If I see a sudden disappearance of Christians, I'll give my life to Jesus."* He was clearly waiting for an outward sign to prove to him that the claims of Christ

---

a See Isaiah 53:3-10.

b John 1:29.

c Luke 24:25-27.

were true and that Christ should be the Lord of his life. Of course, I immediately warned that person that he could die tomorrow and never get that signal.

The point for this study, however, is this, if this foolhardy understanding was isolated to a few intrepid individuals then it would, possibly, not need to be addressed. However, it appears not to be an isolated misconception. Preachers on Christian radio[a] have told their audiences that if they see this sudden disappearance of people then they had better get right with God, and quick! Apocalyptic Christian tracts often communicate the same advice. (A cursory examination of popular Christian books and movies about the second coming exposes the same teaching of a "second-chance" opportunity. In a Christian movie series titled, <u>A Thief in the Night</u>, which was popular in the nineteen seventies/eighties, this "second-chance" message was implicit throughout. It seemed to be one of the primary purposes for the production of these movies.)

Some pretribulationist leaders have even gone so far as to teach or advise that the Church does not need to sponsor extensive missionary work among Jewish groups, because the Jews will not return to Christ until after the Rapture. One teacher on a radio ministry advised that the Christian Church should not waist resources or risk antagonizing Jewish groups for this very reason. One of his main points was that when the Church is raptured the Jews will realize who their Messiah is and will then return to Him in droves.

There is something wrong here. The gospel message must go to the Jew first[b] and should be commended to the conscience all the unsaved solely on the basis of its merits.[c] Namely, man's perilous need and Christ's completed and perfect work. This offering of another chance

---

a Actually I have heard this sentiment expressed several times and by several different persons. It has been heard enough times to cause me to believe that this is a common instruction given by pretribulationists not only to unpersuaded unbelievers, but also to their audiences in general.

b See Romans 1:16.

c See 2 Corinthians 4:2.

to receive Christ when His claims have been proven to the skeptic by this supposed sign of "the disappearance of the Church" is unscriptural, yea, even anti-scriptural. Jesus said, *An evil and adulterous generation seeketh after a sign; and there shall no sign be given to it, but the sign of the prophet Jonas.*[a]

Believers are to commend the gospel to the consciences of their unsaved hearers. There is no sound Biblical justification for offering this message of getting another chance to receive Christ after the Church disappears. In my opinion this understanding has already caused unsaved individuals to believe that they will have another opportunity to accept Christ after His claims have been proven to them by the disappearance of the Church (i.e. the first-second coming of Christ). One person even noted that he understood that the Tribulation period will be a difficult time to get right with God, and then he said, *"But hey, better late than never, I guess."*

---

a Matthew 12:39.

6:   Are the Redeemed Appointed to Wrath?

The Bible declares that *God hath not appointed us to wrath, but to obtain salvation by our Lord Jesus Christ.*[a] Many who hold to the pretribulation Rapture perspective see this promise as evidence that the Church will not go through the Tribulation. They also site this verse against a posttribulational perspective, declaring that a Rapture of the Church after the Tribulation would contradict this reference and would doom the Church to go through the wrath of God.

However, I have never encountered a posttribulationist that believed that the Church will go through the wrath of God. Indeed, most posttribulationists would point to this very verse to categorically proclaim that believers will not go through the wrath.

So, why the confusion? Actually, the confusion lies in a difference of understanding between the two camps regarding the nature of the Great Tribulation.

Pretribulationists generally see the Great Tribulation and the wrath of God as synonymous, or at least that during the Tribulation the fulness of the wrath of God will be outpoured. Typically, their view is that the great trouble of that time will be because of God's outpoured wrath.

Posttribulationists, on the other hand, generally see a marked distinction between the Great Tribulation and the wrath of God. Indeed, though they recognize that there will be targeted releases of wrath during the Tribulation, they teach that the *wrath of the Lamb*[b] will not be fully poured out upon the wicked until after the Great Tribulation. Their view is that wrath will come upon wicked men at the very day of Christ's return. (It should be noted that several Biblical references are quite clear in proclaiming that the full wrath of God, or *of the Lamb,* will not be visited upon the unrepentant until Christ is actually seen coming in the clouds by these wicked individuals.[c])

---

a 1 Thessalonians 5:9.

b Revelation 6:16.

c See Matthew 24:29-30, Jude 1:14-15, & Revelation 1:7, 6:16.

The phrase, ***wrath to come***, primarily refers to damnation. When John the Baptist preached *flee from the wrath to come,*[a] he was calling men to turn off of the road to hell and on to the road to heaven. Finding salvation in Jesus Christ means that we have been saved from wrath. Therefore, it is wholly wrong and scandalous to believe that any redeemed individual will go through the wrath. Wrath and salvation are mutually exclusive. Since it is clear that there will be many saints of God on earth during the Great Tribulation,[b] we must also conclude that the wrath is separate from that Tribulation period. The understanding that the wrath of God will be outpoured when Christ is actually coming in the clouds, illuminates the reason for the instantaneous *change* of the saints. When Christ returns He will come as the King of Righteousness, and His wrath will be visited upon all the ungodly.[c] The redeemed, however, will be pulled out of that conflagration in the same way that righteous Lot was spirited away (by angels[d]) from Sodom when God's wrath descended.

The posttribulationist does not believe that Christians will suffer the wrath of God, he believes that Christ will rapidly (***in the twinkling of an eye***[e]) Rapture His Church out of the wrath when He appears in the clouds. However, he does believe that prior to Christ's return Christians will go through the Great Tribulation.

Romans 5:9 - Much more then, being now justified by his blood, we shall be saved from wrath through him.

1 Thessalonians 1:10 - And to wait for his Son from heaven, whom he raised from the dead, even Jesus, which delivered us from the wrath to come.

---

a Matthew 3:7, Luke 3:7.

b See Revelation 6:9-11, 7:9, 13-14, 20:4.

c See Jude 1:14-15.

d By angels. See Genesis 19:15-16, Matthew 13:30, 39, 24:31, & Mark 13:27.

e 1 Corinthians 15:52.

1 Thessalonians 5:9 - For God hath not appointed us to wrath, but to obtain salvation by our Lord Jesus Christ,

Each of these three verses establish beyond question that believers will not go through the wrath of God. If, however, the Great Tribulation and the wrath are synonymous, as many claim, then it must also be concluded that all the Tribulation saints will suffer the wrath of God. That necessary conclusion of the pretribulationists' doctrinal position, however, not only violates the obvious meaning of these texts, it also insults the essence of redemption. No redeemed individual is appointed to wrath. If a person is born again during the Great Tribulation, then he has *obtain*[ed] *salvation by our Lord Jesus Christ.* Therefore, he is delivered *from the wrath to come.* But if the Great Tribulation is *the wrath to come*, then Tribulation saints will go through the wrath. How can this be? Are they not *saved from wrath through him*?![a]

God has promised the redeemed of the Lord that He *hath not appointed us to wrath, but to obtain salvation by our Lord Jesus Christ.* So is God planning millions of raptures? He must be, if the Tribulation is *the wrath to come.* Every time someone is born again during the Great Tribulation he will need to be raptured out of the wrath, for the redeemed are not appointed to wrath!!

It is interesting that those who argue that Christians cannot go through the Great Tribulation because it is the *wrath to come*, seem to have no problem consigning all the innumerable host of Tribulation saints to that wrath of God. John describes one host of Tribulation saints in this way: *After this I beheld, and, lo, a great multitude, which no man could number, of all nations, and kindreds, and people, and tongues, stood before the throne, and before the Lamb, clothed with white robes, and palms in their hands; And cried with a loud voice, saying, Salvation to our God which sitteth upon the throne, and unto the Lamb... And one of the elders answered, saying unto me, What are these which are arrayed in white robes? and whence came they? And I said unto him, Sir, thou knowest. And he said to me,*

---

a Romans 5:9

These are they which came out of great tribulation, and have washed their robes, and made them white in the blood of the Lamb.[a] (Note, this description certainly sounds like a description of the Church of Jesus Christ[b] and it is clearly noted that they *came out of great tribulation* by martyrdom.)

It is inconsistent to say that one group of people that have been saved by the blood of Christ (read, the Church) cannot go through the wrath of God, while also maintaining that a host of other people who have been saved by the blood of Christ (read, Tribulation saints) can and will go through that wrath.[c] The plain truth is that no believer will go through the wrath of God! Therefore, the Great Tribulation is not the wrath of God and any wrath that will be visited on man at that time will be limited and distinctly targeted to the ungodly, and the righteous will be shielded from it.

Looking at this debate from another perspective, it should be clear to the Bible student that the Great Tribulation period is not the *wrath to come.* The Great Tribulation is described in the Bible as being a time of great persecution, of devastating world wars, of dreadful and theretofore unheard of natural disasters, of increased demonic and supernatural activity, and of God's judgments. Yet the Bible believing Christian must realize that even all these horrors cannot compare to the brimstone fire of the wrath of God. The fire of God's wrath is the fire of hell, no living human experience, regardless of how dreadful, can compare to the torments of hell-fire wrath.

Notice how this is described in Matthew 24. The Scripture states, *Immediately after the tribulation of those days shall the sun be darkened, and the moon shall not give her light, and the stars shall fall from heaven, and the powers of the heavens shall be shaken: And*

---

a Revelation 7:9-10, 13-14.

b Many pretribulationists teach that there is no mention of the Church in the book of Revelation after chapter three.

c Please note, I do not make a distinction between the Church of Christ and the Tribulation saints, but pretribulationists do. Chapter 15 will deal more thoroughly with this separating of the redeemed by the pretribulationists.

then shall appear the sign of the Son of man in heaven: and then shall all the tribes of the earth mourn, and they shall see the Son of man coming in the clouds of heaven with power and great glory.[a] The Lord proclaimed here that after the **tribulation of those days** He will appear in the clouds. It is then when **all the tribes of the earth mourn**. These regretful mourners have already endured the Great Tribulation, yet they are terrified by the specter of God's wrath which is coming upon them. When Jesus returns to earth, He will come as a Holy Judge. He will then destroy the enemies of righteousness with His wrath.

The description of the Lord's triumphal return recorded in Revelation 19 makes it clear that the **wrath of Almighty God**[b] is a distinct component of His return. (*And I saw heaven opened, and behold a white horse; and he that sat upon him was called Faithful and True, and in righteousness he doth judge and make war. His eyes were as a flame of fire, and on his head were many crowns; and he had a name written, that no man knew, but he himself. And he was clothed with a vesture dipped in blood: and his name is called The Word of God. And the armies which were in heaven followed him upon white horses, clothed in fine linen, white and clean. And out of his mouth goeth a sharp sword, that with it he should smite the nations: and he shall rule them with a rod of iron: and he treadeth the winepress of the fierceness and wrath of Almighty God. And he hath on his vesture and on his thigh a name written, KING OF KINGS, AND LORD OF LORDS. And I saw an angel standing in the sun; and he cried with a loud voice, saying to all the fowls that fly in the midst of heaven, Come and gather yourselves together unto the supper of the great God; That ye may eat the flesh of kings, and the flesh of captains, and the flesh of mighty men, and the flesh of horses, and of them that sit on them, and the flesh of all men, both free and bond, both small and great. And I saw the beast, and the kings of the earth, and their armies, gathered together to make war against him that sat on the horse, and against his army. And the beast was taken, and with*

---

a Matthew 24:29-30.

b Revelation 19:15.

him the false prophet that wrought miracles before him, with which he deceived them that had received the mark of the beast, and them that worshipped his image. These both were cast alive into a lake of fire burning with brimstone.[a]) This *fierceness and wrath* is the very thing that causes such terror in the camp of the enemies of Christ!

A distinct fact is clearly proclaimed in many of the passages that describe the return of Christ. That fact? When Christ comes He will come as the worlds judge, and will bring with Him the wrath of Almighty God! Jude states it quite emphatically: *Behold, the Lord cometh with ten thousands of his saints, To execute judgment upon all, and to convince all that are ungodly among them of all their ungodly deeds which they have ungodly committed, and of all their hard speeches which ungodly sinners have spoken against him.*[b] A particular purpose for the coming of the Lord will be to meet out wrath.

It is appropriate here for me to acknowledge a passage that clearly speaks of the wrath of God being poured out during the Great Tribulation. That passage is the description of the dispensing of the *seven golden vials full of the wrath of God*[c] recorded in Revelation chapters 15 and 16. As a posttribulationist, I readily affirm two distinct truths about this passage. First, it is clearly a pouring out of God's wrath. And second, it occurs during the Great Tribulation.

Having affirmed those truths some other truths should also be affirmed. Notice that this passage makes it clear that these *vials full of the wrath* are used to deliver targeted wrath to particular groups of wicked individuals. This specific *wrath* is only visited upon the wicked followers of the beast. This targeted outpouring is similar in type to the hell-fire wrath that was visited upon the cities of Sodom and Gomorrah[d] in Abraham's day. These individuals have already received the mark of the beast which is their sign of allegiance to Satan and the Antichrist.

a Revelation 19:11-20.

b Jude 1:14-15.

c Revelation 15:7.

d See Genesis 19:24.

They have said their final no to Christ's offer of salvation and are therefore *twice dead, plucked up by the roots*.[a] It is quite clear that these wicked men will receive the wrath of God and receive it during the Tribulation. Yet, be careful to note that this is a very specialized visitation of wrath, and it is not the final wrath that comes upon the beast and his followers at the return of Christ. It is for a particular group of people. The rest of the world, and especially the redeemed are shielded from this wrath.

Events like this, though rare, are not unheard of in redemptive history. The wrath which was visited on Sodom and Gomorrah[b] is the preeminent Scriptural example. Along with Sodom and Gomorrah, though, there are other Biblical references of the wrath of Almighty God being delivered in a targeted way. During their sojourn in the wilderness certain of the children of Israel who lusted for meat were visited with wrath.[c] Also, there is implication that the cities of Tyre and Zidon (Sidon)[d] were destroyed by targeted wrath. There are other examples as well. These outpourings, however, are entirely directed at a particular group of wicked people. It still remains that the general visitation of wrath that will come upon the wicked is reserved for a period immediately following the Great Tribulation, when Jesus is visibly returning in the clouds.

In summary, the Bible reveals that when Jesus returns, He will come with wrath to be poured out on Satan, the Antichrist, the false prophet, and all men who have rejected Christ's salvation offer. This will be incomprehensibly worse than any of the horrors of the Great Tribulation. In Revelation six, at the opening of the sixth seal, wicked men on earth have already endured much of the Great Tribulation, yet they say *to the mountains and rocks, Fall on us, and hide us from the face of him that sitteth on the throne, and from the wrath of the*

---

a Jude 1:12.

b Genesis 19:24-25.

c See Psalm 78:30-31.

d See Matthew 11:21-22.

Lamb.[a] They will not fear death they will fear Christ's holy face and His wrath. The horrors of the Great Tribulation are largely perpetrated by wicked men and devils, but wrath will be brought by Almighty God! Therefore, it is clear that the Great Tribulation and God's wrath are not synonymous.

---

a Revelation 6:16.

7:   Sealing the Saints of God

Although, as was seen in the previous chapter, the ***wrath of the Lamb***[a] will not be poured out until the Lamb is actually coming in the clouds of heaven, the Tribulation period does include many judgments from God (and also limited or targeted wrath.) *Judgment*, in Scripture, usually refers to chastisement that God brings in order to turn men from their wicked way.   God's judgment is for the Church as well as the world.   In truth, the Bible states that ***the time is come that judgment must begin at the house of God.***[b]   God judges both His Church and unbelievers to cause transgressors to turn from evil and cry out to God for mercy through the merits of Christ's redemption.   There is still hope of redemption in judgment.   In fact, the malefactor's repentance is the primary reason that God sends judgment.

Wrath, on the other hand, usually has a finality attached to it. Wrath is what men receive when they reject judgments.   In its general Biblical usage there is no hope of redemption in wrath.   A verse which demonstrates this distinction between wrath and judgment is found in Proverbs: ***He, that being often reproved*** (judgments) ***hardeneth his neck, shall suddenly be destroyed*** (wrath)***, and that without remedy.***[c]

Though there will be some specialized dispersions of wrath during the Great Tribulation, the primary way that God will work to get the attention of wicked men will be through judgments.   Indeed, along with the raging evils of men and the malevolent and diabolic activity of Satan, the Great Tribulation will include judgments from God.   In these judgments God will purify His Church and give a last offer of salvation to wicked men.   Many of these judgments and all of the targeted wrath, however, will be specifically for the wicked.   In those cases God will shield the righteous as He has done throughout history.

Many criticize the posttribulational position by asserting that, if true, the faithful would then be doomed to pass through all the wrath or

---

a Revelation 6:16.

b 1 Peter 4:17.

c Proverbs 29:1.

judgments of God during the Great Tribulation. Though it is true that the righteous will undergo great persecution[a] and some of the judgments during the Tribulation, it is also true that God will intentionally protect or seal the righteous from much of the calamity of that time. This fact is often overlooked by those of the pretribulation perspective.

We must realize that Christians through the ages have suffered for righteousness' sake, and they continue to suffer to this very day. The blood of the saints has been and is being shed for the cause of Christ, and this at the hands of satanically inspired persecutors. The Great Tribulation period will, of a surety, be an extreme intensification of such satanic persecution, but it will also be a time when believers will be blessed with protection from God in an intensified way. The Lord promises His own, *When thou passest through the waters, I will be with thee; and through the rivers, they shall not overflow thee: when thou walkest through the fire, thou shalt not be burned; neither shall the flame kindle upon thee.*[b]

Notice the distinct shielding promises in the following bulleted list of Scriptures:

- *Psalm 91:1-16 - ¹He that dwelleth in the secret place of the most High shall abide under the shadow of the Almighty. ²I will say of the LORD, He is my refuge and my fortress: my God; in him will I trust. ³Surely he shall deliver thee from the snare of the fowler, and from the noisome pestilence. ⁴He shall cover thee with his feathers, and under his wings shalt thou trust: his truth shall be thy shield and buckler. ⁵Thou shalt not be afraid for the terror by night; nor for the arrow that flieth by day; ⁶Nor for the pestilence that walketh in darkness; nor for the destruction that wasteth at noonday. ⁷A thousand shall fall at thy side, and ten thousand at thy right hand; but it shall not come nigh thee. ⁸Only with thine eyes shalt thou behold and see the reward of the wicked. ⁹Because*

---

a See Revelation 6:9*ff.*

b Isaiah 43:2.

thou hast made the LORD, which is my refuge, even the most High, thy habitation; ¹⁰There shall no evil befall thee, neither shall any plague come nigh thy dwelling. ¹¹For he shall give his angels charge over thee, to keep thee in all thy ways. ¹²They shall bear thee up in their hands, lest thou dash thy foot against a stone. ¹³Thou shalt tread upon the lion and adder: the young lion and the dragon shalt thou trample under feet. ¹⁴Because he hath set his love upon me, therefore will I deliver him: I will set him on high, because he hath known my name. ¹⁵He shall call upon me, and I will answer him: I will be with him in trouble; I will deliver him, and honour him. ¹⁶With long life will I satisfy him, and shew him my salvation.

The prophetic nature of this Psalm must not be overlooked. It applied to our Lord while on earth[a] and it applies to the saints who go through the Great Tribulation. This Psalm proclaims the virtues of the Christian's great "champion God" who will care for and protect His own, even in great tribulation. (*Only with thine eyes shalt thou behold and see the reward of the wicked*.) Christians would do well to memorize Psalm 91 and hold the promises close to heart in coming days. An old Scottish proverb states, *"You cannot thatch your roof in the rain."* Before the storm comes, O Christian, diligently store up God's Word in your heart! God lovingly says to His child, *Because he hath set his love upon me, therefore will I deliver him: I will set him on high, because he hath known my name.* The wonderful promises in this Psalm bring tears of joy to the eye of the child of faith!

▪ *Luke 21:18 - But there shall not an hair of your head perish.*

This is a promise for believers who are actually going through the Great Tribulation. It shows that God is active, not only in judgment, but also in gentle protection during that foreboding time. It is inconsistent

---

a See Matthew 4:6 & Luke 4:10-11.

to claim that God could not shield the Church in judgment (or wrath,) so the Church must be removed, while at the same time maintaining that God will protect the innumerable number of Tribulation saints in judgment. Even if the Tribulation period were the time or day of the outpouring of God's wrath,*a* God would certainly shelter and protect His own in that time. If the Tribulation saints can be shielded from much of the judgments, as the Bible clearly reveals that they will be, then there is no ground to insist that God must remove the Church.

One might ask the question, "Why must the Church be removed?" Is God incapable of protecting His own? Christian's are the precious children of the God of the universe! He says to them, ***Behold, I am the LORD, the God of all flesh: is there any thing too hard for me?***[b] He can and will protect the innumerable host[c] of saints who go through the Great Tribulation.

- ***John 17:15 - I pray not that thou shouldest take them out of the world, but that thou shouldest keep them from the evil.***

God does not promise that He will take the righteous out of the world during trouble. He does, however, promise that He will keep them from evil in the midst of trouble. Persecution is a sure result of following Christ. ***Yea, and all that will live godly in Christ Jesus shall suffer persecution.***[d] The very word, *tribulation*, most often refers in Scripture to what the righteous endure from the wicked for Christ's sake. Jesus said to the Church, ***These things I have spoken unto you, that in me ye might have peace. In the world ye shall have tribulation: but be of good cheer; I have overcome the world.***[e] The Church of Christ will still be in the world during the Great Tribulation, and will continue to be blessed with Christ's overcoming power.

---

a As previously established, the Great Tribulation is not the day of God's wrath.

b Jeremiah 32:27.

c See Revelation 7:9.

d 2 Timothy 3:12.

e John 16:33.

- ***Revelation 7:3 - Saying, Hurt not the earth, neither the sea, nor the trees, till we have sealed the servants of our God in their foreheads.***

In this text the judgment of God is withheld until the **servants of our God** are sealed **in their foreheads**. This sealing apparently does not protect them from martyrdom or Satan's attacks, because Revelation 7:14 reports on the innumerable multitude of believers that are martyred during this time. This sealing does, however, protect these saints from the judgments that God is preparing to release upon the earth. By the redemption of Christ, the redeemed have been saved from wrath. Christians are also specifically told that they may endure persecutions, distresses, hardships, and infirmities perpetrated by the Devil and his cohorts for the name and the cause of Christ. The Bible teaches that suffering is actually God's will for believers so that they may be purged from worldliness and stand as true witnesses of Him. In fact, when Christians suffer righteously they give profound testimony to the deity of Christ. Yet, the Scripture promises Christ beloved, you **are kept by the power of God through faith unto salvation ready to be revealed in the last time. Wherein ye greatly rejoice, though now for a season, if need be, ye are in heaviness through manifold temptations: That the trial of your faith, being much more precious than gold that perisheth, though it be tried with fire, might be found unto the praise and honour and glory at the appearing of Jesus Christ.**[a]

In the time of the Tribulation we see the Church enduring an intensification of persecution led by a devil-possessed Antichrist. Though this picture is not appealing, we must realize that this cannot be the fire and brimstone of the wrath of God. Through the ages believers have suffered horrendous abuses and injustices. Scripture forebodes the increase of these griefs upon Christians up to the very return of the Lord. Did not Christ Jesus tell His followers, **If they have persecuted me, they will also persecute you?**[b] Yet, in all this trouble God is wonderfully protecting His beloved.

---

a 1 Peter 1:5-7.

b John 15:20.

- *Revelation 9:4 - And it was commanded them that they should not hurt the grass of the earth, neither any green thing, neither any tree; but only those men which have not the seal of God in their foreheads.*

In this text the locusts from the pit are only allowed to hurt *those men which have not the seal of God in their foreheads.* Thus, those who have the seal of God are protected.

- *Revelation 16:2 - And the first went, and poured out his vial upon the earth; and there fell a noisome and grievous sore upon the men which had the mark of the beast, and upon them which worshipped his image.*

This judgment comes only *upon the men which had the mark of the beast, and upon them which worshipped his image.* Again, the righteous and possibly even the ignorant and/or undecided are shielded from this judgment.

- *Revelation 18:4 - And I heard another voice from heaven, saying, Come out of her, my people, that ye be not partakers of her sins, and that ye receive not of her plagues.*

The destruction of Mystery Babylon is preceded by a call to the people of God to come out of her *that ye be not partakers of her sins, and that ye receive not of her plagues.* Though this is not an example of God supernaturally removing His people, it is an example of God telling a watchful Church to come out of an area targeted for judgment. By divine action God's people are still delivered from heaven's judgments if they heed the warning to come out. This seems a similar type of shielding from judgment as was given to the Israelites when they were instructed to place the lamb's blood on their doorposts. If they heeded the instructions they were sealed from the judgment.[a]

---

[a] See Exodus 12:13

Some Additional Biblical Examples of Divine Protection:

■ The salvation of Noah and his family is the Scriptural archetype of God's deliverance of the righteous out of wrath.[a] Noah's deliverance is a promise to all the righteous. The Church of God in the last days can take hope, knowing a sure deliverance will come.

It is very important to realize that Noah's deliverance did not precede the outpouring of God's wrath, they occurred *in the selfsame day.* The Bible states, *In the six hundredth year of Noah's life, in the second month, the seventeenth day of the month, the same day were all the fountains of the great deep broken up, and the windows of heaven were opened.*[b] Concerning the day the flood came, the Word very specifically states, *In the selfsame day entered Noah, and Shem, and Ham, and Japheth, the sons of Noah, and Noah's wife, and the three wives of his sons with them, into the ark.*[c]

The Bible student should recognize that God has always delivered the righteous out of wrath. However, the Great Tribulation is identified by the Lord Himself as being a particularly terrible time, not because of God's wrath, but because of the attacks of the wicked. The Lord's wrath, as seen in the previous chapter, is very specifically identified to come from God and will be exclusively for the wicked.

■ Lot, his wife, and two daughters were speedily spirited away from Sodom by angels at the very moment the fire and brimstone shower was descending upon those wicked cities.[d] This is a Biblical example of how Christ will Rapture His Church out of the wrath after the Great Tribulation. Jesus has proclaimed that His angels will once again be summoned to this holy work of removing the righteous out of hell-fire wrath. Immediately after the Great Tribulation[e] the angels will gather

---

a See Genesis 7:1*ff.*

b Genesis 7:11.

c Genesis 7:13.

d See Genesis 19:15-16.

e See Matthew 24:29.

the Church in the air. This occurs at Christ's coming[a] and when the wrath of God is falling.

  ▪ Joseph received a revelation from God which enabled him to prepare for the seven lean years.[b] This seven year famine is, most certainly, a prophetic foreshadowing of the seven year Tribulation period. Therefore, God's characteristic means of delivering the *righteous... out of trouble*[c] is by providential protection and heavenly supply. However, deliverance by physical removal only happens in wrath.

  ▪ Prior to the Exodus the children of Israel experienced God's shielding protection from many of Egypt's plagues.[d] Though they dwelt in the same country, the Israelites did not suffer like the Egyptians. In some of the plagues the Israelites were blessed with God's covering,[e] in others God sent a preparative warning through His prophet, Moses.[f] Even the word, *passover,*[g] speaks of God protecting or shielding His people in judgment. Notice that they were protected from God's judgment, but they were not protected from all trouble. Their taskmasters were more severe, they had to glean straw by night for their brick-making,[h] and they experienced a general increase in trouble and hardship.[i]

  ▪ While in the wilderness, the Israelites were cared for and protected in profound and special ways. When thirsty, God provided fresh-flowing water from a rock for their relief.[j] They were fed with angel's food from heaven.[k] Their clothes and shoes were given divine

---

a See Matthew 24:31 & Mark 13:27.

b See Genesis 41:25-32.

c Proverbs 11:8.

d See Exodus 8:22-23, 9:4, 26, 10:23.

e Ibid.

f See Exodus 12:21-23.

g See Exodus 12:11, 21, 27, 43, 48.

h See Exodus 5:7-9.

i See Exodus 6:9.

j See Exodus 17:6.

k See Exodus 16:35 & Psalm 78:24-25.

durability.[a] Supernatural and overcoming power was given to their armies.[b] In general, they lacked nothing![c] This was a host of people that numbered in the millions. They were traveling through one of the most barren regions on the surface of the earth. Yet, God miraculously provided water, food, clothing, and shelter. How can one doubt God's shielding and sustaining promises and capabilities?!

  ▪ Elijah was providentially nourished and sheltered during a 3½ year drought.[d] Again, the timing of this drought seems a prophetic antecedent to the last half of the Tribulation period and a prophetic testimony of God's rescuing power. In the prophetic books of Daniel[e] and Revelation[f] the Tribulation is divided into two 3½ year periods. The first is a time of growing world troubles, the second is a time of great tribulation. God has left His Church witness in the life of His holy prophet, Elijah, that He will care for His people even in great tribulation. God performed many miracles during this care for Elijah including commanding ravens[g] to feed him.

  ▪ Shadrach, Meshach, and Abednego were miraculously safeguarded while going through intense fire.[h] Is that not a distinct promise that God is able to protect His faithful Church?! Is anything more powerful than God's sustaining grace? O believer, may God help you to rely upon His victorious care in these last days. For *"He is able to deliver thee!"*

  ▪ In Daniel's thrilling deliverance from harm while in the very midst of the lions' den[i] there is verification of God's promise to the redeemed! (***He shall call upon me, and I will answer him: I will be***

---

a See Deuteronomy 8:4, 29:5.

b See Exodus 12:10-12.

c See Deuteronomy 2:7.

d See 1 Kings 17:1-24.

e See Daniel 9:27.

f See Revelation 11:3, 12:6.

g See 1 Kings 17:4-6.

h See Daniel 3:19-26.

i See Daniel 6:22.

with him in trouble; I will deliver him, and honour him.[a]) God can do the impossible, and He has left ample testimony to assure Christians that He intends to do just that in their behalf during the Great Tribulation.

■ Peter was miraculously delivered from prison and led safely through hostile forces by the angel of the Lord.[b] Christians serve the same Savior today!

■ Paul was divinely protected and cared for on several occasions.[c] The "Apostle to the Gentiles" bore testimony of the Lord's sustaining care with these words: *For we would not, brethren, have you ignorant of our trouble which came to us in Asia, that we were pressed out of measure, above strength, insomuch that we despaired even of life: But we had the sentence of death in ourselves, that we should not trust in ourselves, but in God which raiseth the dead: Who delivered us from so great a death, and doth deliver: in whom we trust that he will yet deliver us.*[d] Dear Christian, you can also be assured that Christ will *yet deliver* you.

Many other examples could be referenced, but these examples should be sufficient to illustrate the fact that God is able to protect His own and intends to do just that during the Great Tribulation. In many of the judgments of that day, God will shield His faithful bride, but in all of the judgments of that day God will sustain her.

Please note also that in the life of each of these Bible heros we have example of how the righteous often suffer and *are persecuted for righteousness' sake.*[e] Christians should keep these two realities distinctly before them: Christ's redemption assures that we are protected from wrath, but we are expressly called to partake in His sufferings.

During the Great Tribulation God will protect the elect from the brunt of His judgments, but He also tells the elect that they will have

---

a Psalm 93:15.

b See Acts 12:6-11.

c See Acts 28:3-5 & 2 Corinthians 11:23-27.

d 2 Corinthians 1:8-10.

e Matthew 5:10.

tribulation and persecution in this world. For this reason the precious words of Christ must be held firm. On the night of His betrayal Jesus told the disciples of the coming trouble. He also reassured them of His great love for them and of His overcoming power. Christ's then gave these precious words of comfort to the redeemed, ***These things I have spoken unto you, that in me ye might have peace. In the world ye shall have tribulation: but be of good cheer; I have overcome the world.***[a]

---

a John 16:33.

8:   A Restrainer of Evil Is Removed

2 Thessalonians 2:6-7 - ⁶And now ye know what withholdeth that he might be revealed in his time. ⁷For the mystery of iniquity doth already work: only he who now letteth will let, until he be taken out of the way.

A curious teaching has emerged in the pretribulationists' camp surrounding this text which merits a thorough examination. Many have extracted from verse seven a teaching about the timing of the Rapture which seems wholly unsupported by the text. The idea is that the removed restrainer, or *he who now letteth*,[a] must refer to the Holy Spirit. Also it is understood that being *taken out of the way* means that the Holy Ghost will be completely removed from the earth. Further, His removal must then also include the Church's removal from earth, because the Holy Spirit would not leave the earth without taking the Church with Him. Since Christ *hath said, I will never leave thee, nor forsake thee*,[b] then it follows, according to this theory, that the Church will be removed when the restraining Holy Spirit is removed.

From a tiny foundation of someone being *taken out of the way* of the *mystery of iniquity* an elaborate pretribulation Rapture edifice has been erected. Many pretribulationists will site this text as their primary proof that the Church will not go through the Great Tribulation. Yet, the context of this verse expressly directs these Gentile Christians to expect the *man of sin* to be revealed before Christ gathers His Church unto Him.[c] Nevertheless, pretribulationists state emphatically that, in light of verse seven, the Church will not be on earth when the Antichrist is revealed (i.e. the *mystery of iniquity* is unleashed). They strongly claim that verse seven settles the matter. Their conclusion? The only way to remove the restrainer (*he who now letteth*) is to remove the

---

a This is an archaic usage. The term, *'let,'* means here: *to hold back, hinder, impede, prevent.* Webster's New International Dictionary, pg. 1419.

b Hebrews 13:5.

c See 2 Thessalonians 2:1-3.

Church. Therefore, they contend that the Rapture of the Church must take place before the ***man of sin*** (Antichrist) is revealed.

It should first be observed that the extrapolations of doctrine taken from verse seven by pretribulationists seem at best excessive, and may even constitute a grave adding to the Word of God. The Rapture of the Church is not the focus of these two verses, but rather the insidious ***mystery of iniquity***, and the coming time when a restrainer of this iniquity will no longer hold it back. When the one who now restrains this iniquity is removed (***taken out of the way***) certainly evil will explode onto the world scene. This evil is specifically connected to and will assuredly be concentrated in the person of the Antichrist. However, there is no textual justification for claiming that the Church is not present on earth during this time.

Notice also that there is no indication in this passage that the Holy Spirit is the restrainer here (***he who now letteth***.) The verse does not seem to be referring to God at all, but rather to some servant of God. The Holy Ghost, of course, is not God's servant, He is God! The restrainer referenced here is ***taken out of the way***, or ordered out of the way. It seems a reach to believe that the Holy Spirit would move the apostle Paul to refer to Himself in that manner.

There is another candidate for this unidentified restrainer; the archangel Michael. It seems much more probable that he is the servant of God referenced here. Several prophetic texts indicate that this restrainer (***he who now letteth***) is, indeed, the archangel Michael. He is specifically identified several times in Scripture as the one who is assigned to restrain Satan and impede his machinations. In the prophetic books of Daniel,[a] Jude,[b] and Revelation[c] the archangel Michael is the designated champion of the people of God and he has the particular task of countering Satan and resisting his evil influence.

There are also several references in Revelation that describe other angelic beings releasing or unleashing evil or calamity on to the earth.

---

a See Daniel 10:13, 21, 12:1.

b See Jude 1:9.

c See Revelation 12:7.

Examples include, the breaking of the seals of the seven-sealed book,[a] the seven trumpet judgments,[b] and the seven vials of wrath.[c] Notice the distinctiveness of these releasing events, as recorded at the sounding of the sixth trumpet: *And the sixth angel sounded, and I heard a voice from the four horns of the golden altar which is before God, Saying to the sixth angel which had the trumpet, <u>Loose the four angels which are bound in the great river Euphrates. And the four angels were loosed, which were prepared for an hour, and a day, and a month, and a year, for to slay the third part of men. And the number of the army of the horsemen were two hundred thousand thousand: and I heard the number of them.</u>*[d]

Yet the student of Scripture should recognize that this 2 Thessalonians passage does not specifically identify *he who now letteth.* What we do know about him is that he restrains the *mystery of iniquity* until he is *taken out of the way.* Unless the Church is *he who now letteth,* nothing is said or even implied here about the removal of the Church. The restrainer could, of course, be the Church. However, the masculine pronoun, "*he,*" makes that interpretation unlikely.

Furthermore, even if the restrainer is the Holy Ghost or the Church, there is no justification for saying that the restrainer is taken out of the earth. The text merely states that the restrainer is *taken out of the <u>way</u>* of the *mystery of iniquity.* Nothing is said about this restrainer being removed from the planet!

The Holy Spirit must be present and active in the world during the Tribulation, because an innumerable host will be saved in those days.[e] Jesus said, *Except a man be born of water and of the Spirit, he cannot enter into the kingdom of God.*[f] The Bible also clearly affirms that *if*

---

a See Revelation 6:1-17, 8:1-2.

b See Revelation 8:3-10:7, 11:15.

c See Revelation 15:7-16:21.

d Revelation 9:13-16.

e See Revelation 7:9-14.

f John 3:5.

any man have not the Spirit of Christ, he is none of his.[a] Therefore, the presence of redeemed people on earth during the Great Tribulation verifies beyond question that the Holy Spirit will still be present and active on earth during that time. No one can confess Christ but by the Holy Ghost, as the Bible emphatically states; ***no man can say that Jesus is the Lord, but by the Holy Ghost.***[b]

The curious and excessive assumptions made by some pretribulationists from these two verses are even more apparent when the entire context of this passage is considered. Pretribulationists usually teach that the Antichrist will not be revealed until after the Rapture of the Church. They use 2 Thessalonians 2:7 as their proof-text for this teaching. Yet, 2 Thessalonians 2:1-3 emphatically states that the Rapture (***our gathering*** - vs 1) will not occur until the Antichrist (***that man of sin*** - vs. 3) is revealed. By strained and undue assumptions concerning ***he who now letteth***, many have been led to disregard the plain statement of the greater context of this passage. Who has authorized this type of textual license? Certainly not the Lord nor His Word! Liberties have been taken with this verse that are textually and rationally unjustified.

Furthermore, there is a grave danger latent in any teaching that guarantees Christians that they will not be present on earth when the Antichrist is revealed. God has commanded us to seek spiritual discernment and to identify the ***man of sin***. But if a believer thinks the evil one will not appear until after he has left the earth in the Rapture, then he will naturally not seek to identify this evil one, and, therefore, is liable to be deceived by this great deceiver!

I am of the opinion that many of the teachings found in pretribulationism emerge out of shadowy textual contrivances rather than the plain statements of the text. Elaborate assumptions and suppositions are built upon speculations or "senses" of the text rather than the actual statements of the texts. Teachers state things like, *"The sense in Matthew 24:29-31 is different than that in 1 Thessalonians*

---

a Romans 8:9.

b 1 Corinthians 12:3.

4:15-17." It is interesting that the actual words of these two texts are quite similar. As was noted in chapter 1, both texts reveal that the Lord will descend from heaven and the sound of a trumpet will precede a gathering of the elect in the air. They are assuredly parallel texts which describe the same event. It is true that the Matthew text focuses on how the coming of Christ will affect the earth's inhabitants in general, whereas the 1 Thessalonians text specifically describes how this event will affect believers. But it should be readily recognized that the same event is being described.

When confronted with these seemingly unjustified inferences and the tentative Scriptural nature of their doctrine, many pretribulationists will defend their position by claiming that the pretribulation Rapture is a *"mystery doctrine"*[a] of Scripture. Doubtless, some who hold this view must believe that God has not openly revealed His truth about the Lord's return in His Word. This is certainly erroneous. Not only has God revealed the truth, He has promised heavenly wisdom and understanding of this truth to all who seek it in simple faith.

In summary, there is a day coming when the great **mystery of iniquity** will be fully unleashed upon earth. However, there is no Scriptural justification for the claim that Christian believers will be removed from earth before or at this time. It is left, then, for believers to prepare to stand in that evil day. God's Word leaves believers with this clear command, **Wherefore take unto you the whole armour of God, that ye may be able to withstand <u>in the evil day</u>, and having done all, to stand. Stand therefore, having your loins girt about with truth, and having on the breastplate of righteousness; And your feet shod with the preparation of the gospel of peace; Above all, taking the shield of faith, wherewith ye shall be able to quench all the fiery darts of the wicked. And take the helmet of salvation, and the sword of the Spirit, which is the word of God: Praying always with all prayer and supplication in the Spirit, and watching thereunto with all perseverance and supplication for all saints.**[b]

---

a This *"mystery doctrine"* defense will be examined in chapter 14.

b Ephesians 6:13-18.

9:   That Great Gettin' Up Mornin'

In the hopeful Negro Spiritual titled, "In Dat Great Gettin' Up Mornin'," there is a precious depiction of the hope of the Christian Church. This spiritual, rising from the hearts of believers who were living under the tyranny of slavery and racial discrimination, celebrates and rejoices in the hope of the resurrection. Like few other groups of believers, these subjects of the depravation of slavery and racial bigotry, have articulated the sublime hope of the resurrection of the redeemed. On that glorious day all the forces of injustice and hatred will lose forever their power to oppress and defile. The resurrection of the redeemed is the great deliverance day. It is the day of final redemption, the redemption of the body.

Those sleeping saints, of course, that will be on that particular morning resurrected will already have been relieved by death into the presence of Christ in spirit. Yet, the day of the resurrection is inseparably connected in Holy Writ to not only the day of the bodily resurrection of those who sleep in the faith, but also deliverance to those living saints who are cruelly beset by persecutions and distresses.

In many texts of scripture, this great hope is pictured as the consummate moment of triumph for oppressed believers, and the final act of redemption for all believers, both the quick and the dead. The pressing question though is when this promised resurrection will come. The evident message implied or expressed in the passages that speak of this triumphal morning is that the resurrection will come in the darkest of hours. It is as the old axiom indicates, *"the darkest hour is just before dawn."* So, it seems that the darkest hour of Christian history will be just before the dawn of the resurrection.

The following text is very definitive as to the timing of the resurrection. Indeed it is a cardinal text for establishing the timing of the Rapture of the Church:

Revelation 20:4-6 - ⁴And I saw thrones, and they sat upon them, and
judgment was given unto them: and I saw the souls of them that

*were beheaded for the witness of Jesus, and for the word of God,
and which had not worshipped the beast, neither his image,
neither had received his mark upon their foreheads, or in their
hands; and they lived and reigned with Christ a thousand years.*
*⁵But the rest of the dead lived not again until the thousand years
were finished. This is the first resurrection. ⁶Blessed and holy is
he that hath part in the first resurrection: on such the second
death hath no power, but they shall be priests of God and of
Christ, and shall reign with him a thousand years.*

In this passage the first resurrection, the resurrection of the
righteousness, is identified. The resurrection mentioned here very
definitely occurs after the Great Tribulation for it includes Tribulation
saints. That fact is very significant since it is sure that a resurrection of
the redeemed takes place at the Rapture. So if the Rapture occurs
before this resurrection than there will be a resurrection of the righteous
before the *first resurrection* of the righteous!

But how could that be possible? God's holy Word has specifically
defined the resurrection described in Revelation 20:4-6 as the *first
resurrection*, and that resurrection is declared to occur after the time of
the Great Tribulation. Yet if the Rapture had already occurred before
the Great Tribulation than there would have also been a resurrection
before the one defined in Revelation 20.

So if *first* does not mean *first* then what does it mean? Is not the
meaning of words lost if we can't trust *first* to mean *first*? Surely God
would not have called this resurrection *the first resurrection* if it was
anything other than *the first resurrection*, would He? The Bible says,
Blessed and holy is he that hath part in the first resurrection. This is
the resurrection that Christians believers who have died in the faith are
blessed to participate in.

Please do not miss this vital point. It is sure that a resurrection of
the dead occurs at the Rapture of the Church.[a] It is also sure, from this
text, that the Scripturally defined *first resurrection* will occur after the

---

a See 1 Corinthians 15:51-52 & 1 Thessalonians 4:15-17.

great tribulation and will include believers who have been martyred during the great tribulation. Therefore, the Rapture must happen after the Great Tribulation. The only other resurrection referred to in this chapter will occur after the millennial reign of Christ and is the resurrection of the wicked. (***And I saw the dead, small and great, stand before God; and the books were opened: and another book was opened, which is the book of life: and the dead were judged out of those things which were written in the books, according to their works. And the sea gave up the dead which were in it; and death and hell delivered up the dead which were in them: and they were judged every man according to their works. And death and hell were cast into the lake of fire. This is the second death.***[a]) There is a distinct absence of a resurrection occurring before the Tribulation.

Thus, the Word of God declares with certainty that there are two resurrections that involve mankind and both will occur after the Great Tribulation. From this text we can establish with certainty whether the Rapture of the Church will occur before or after the Great Tribulation. Included in the ***first resurrection*** are believers who were ***beheaded for the witness of Jesus, and for the word of God, and which had not worshipped the beast, neither his image, neither had received his mark upon their foreheads.***[b] The particular events that these Christian martyrs endured only take place during the Great Tribulation. It is only during the Great Tribulation that believers will be beheaded for not receiving the mark of the beast. So it is established beyond question that the ***first resurrection*** will transpire after the Great Tribulation.

Some have objected to reading too much into the term, ***first***, by asserting that the resurrection of the Lord Jesus Christ occurred long before the ***first resurrection*** of Revelation 20. However, this is not a fitting comparison. The resurrections of Revelation 20 are dealing with fallen humans. The resurrection of our Lord Jesus Christ is not. He is the man ***Who did no sin, neither was guile found in his mouth.***[c] His

---

a Revelation 20:12-14.

b Revelation 20:4.

c 1 Peter 2:22.

resurrection is distinct from and genitive to the resurrection of the redeemed. Jesus Christ *is **the head of the body, the church: who is the beginning, the firstborn from the dead; that in all things he might have the preeminence.***[a] As such, His resurrection is separate from comparative numerations.

It is the transparent fact of Revelation 20 that there are two resurrections that involve fallen humanity and both occur after the Great Tribulation. The first is the resurrection of the righteous (redeemed). This fact is categorically established from this text.

Therefore, either the resurrection defined in Revelation 20:4-6 is the fist resurrection of mankind or the Bible is errant. Since **the Bible is not errant**, then the resurrection and Rapture of the Church is unequivocally shown to occur at the return of Christ and after the Great Tribulation.

The placement of this event in the Revelation should also be noted. Both the ***marriage supper of the Lamb***[b] and the ***first resurrection***[c] are described as taking place at the end of John the Apostle's record and after all the descriptions of the Great Tribulation period have been concluded. Though it is true that there is often a repeating of events in Revelation and the narrative is not always following a time order, it still remains that the placement of these events seems curious if indeed they will occur much earlier. If, as some claim, this resurrection will precede the Great Tribulation, would it not have been prophetically recorded in a much earlier chapter? Those who believe that the Rapture will occur before the Great Tribulation, and that the ***marriage supper*** will take place during the Great Tribulation, would do well to consider that the placement of these events in the prophetic record argues against that understanding.

Finally, I am willing to risk redundancy here, to reemphasize the significant place this text holds in defining the timing of the Rapture.

---

a Colossians 1:18.

b Revelation 19:9.

c Revelation 20:5, 6.

The Bible expressly declares that at the Rapture *the dead in Christ shall rise first.*[a] The Bible also expressly declares here that this *first resurrection* will include Great Tribulation saints. The only way to reconcile these two very definitive declarations is to see that the resurrection that will occur at the Rapture is this *first resurrection* and it will take place after the Great Tribulation. Indeed, it is hard to read any other meaning into this, and it is difficult to see how the timing of the *first resurrection* could be any more clearly stated in God's Word!

---

[a] 1 Thessalonians 4:16.

10:   Thoughts on Imminence

An oft used censure of posttribulationism is that its tenets destroy the doctrine of the "imminent return of Christ." This concern certainly merits a response. By this "imminent" terminology, pretribulationists mean that the Scriptures declare a sudden and unannounced return of Christ to Rapture His Church. Therefore, to them any teaching that asserts that certain sings must precede Christ's coming for His Church, of necessity, contradicts this Scriptural instruction about the Rapture.

To begin my answer to this concern and since the word, "imminent," is not used in Scripture, it is appropriate to establish its definition. Implicit in the term, *imminent*, is a sense of nearness and surety. Its primary meaning involves the certainty and immediacy of some event. For example, the statement, *"you saved me from imminent disaster,"* means that had no intervention come, soon and certain disaster would have come. Webster's first and second entries on *imminent* read as follows: *1. Threatening to occur immediately; near at hand; impending; — said esp. of misfortune or peril. "In danger imminent." Spencer. 2. Projecting over or forward; overhanging. "Old stone cities, imminent on the windy seaboard." Stevenson.*[a] Hence, as the terms *"threatening"* and *"projecting"* indicate, *imminence* in its primary usage apparently includes some form of distinct forewarning. When the sky is clear and the sun is shining we would not say a thunderstorm is imminent. That designation would only be given if the sky were dark with thunderclouds. So it is with the return of Christ and the Rapture, when the signs of His return are present then His return is imminent and not until then. This truth was most clearly stated by the Lord: *When it is evening, ye say, It will be fair weather: for the sky is red. And in the morning, It will be foul weather to day: for the sky is red and lowering. O ye hypocrites, ye can discern the face of the sky; but can ye not discern the signs of the times?*[b]

Therefore, if the doctrine of the imminent return of Christ merely advances the surety of the Lord's return and its nearness in relation to

---

a <u>Webster's New International Dictionary</u>, pg. 1245.

b Matthew 16:2-3

clear signs, then the posttribulationist will wholeheartedly embrace it. If, however, the doctrine promotes an understanding that Christ's return to Rapture His Church must happen without warning and no signs will precede it, then he must reject that teaching as unbiblical.

Most who hold to a pretribulation Rapture assert that the Rapture of the Church is imminent, but Christ's bodily return is not. By this designation they mean that the Rapture must happen without warning and will have no preceding signs. Much is made of this understanding in the whole of their doctrinal persuasion. The understanding that Christ will return for the Church without signs or warning is viewed as a great motivation for the Christian's perpetual readiness. (Please note, I firmly believe that Christians must abide in perpetual readiness!)

However, an analysis of the texts of Scripture from which the doctrine of the "imminent return of Christ" is based, reveals that these texts are dealing with Christ's bodily return to earth. Pretribulationists believe that Christ's bodily return to earth is preceded by many signs, not the least of which is their assertion that the Rapture of the Church will have already occurred at least seven years prior. Therefore, it cannot be established from these "imminent return texts" that no signs will precede Christ's coming for the Church. These texts include His bodily return to earth, they list many signs that will precede Christ's bodily return, and warn of a surprise only to the unprepared. Since the Scriptural texts on "*imminence*" primarily focus on Christ's return to earth and include signs to watch for, then it follows that a Scripturally based doctrine of the return of Christ or the Rapture of the Church cannot deny precursory signs.

It should also be noted that some of the most distinct *"imminent return"* passages are found in the Olivet Discourse,[a] which is usually dismissed by pretribulationists as not applying to the Christian Church.[b]

Matthew 24:42-51 - *[42] Watch therefore: for ye know not what hour your Lord doth come. [43] But know this, that if the goodman of the house had known in what watch the thief would come, he would have watched, and would not have suffered his house to be broken*

---

a The Olivet Discourse is recorded in Matthew 24 & 25, Mark 13, & Luke 21.

b The exclusion of the Olivet Discourse will be discussed further in chapter 12.

up. ⁴⁴Therefore be ye also ready: for in such an hour as ye think not the Son of man cometh. ⁴⁵Who then is a faithful and wise servant, whom his lord hath made ruler over his household, to give them meat in due season? ⁴⁶Blessed is that servant, whom his lord when he cometh shall find so doing. ⁴⁷Verily I say unto you, That he shall make him ruler over all his goods. ⁴⁸But and if that evil servant shall say in his heart, My lord delayeth his coming; ⁴⁹And shall begin to smite his fellowservants, and to eat and drink with the drunken; ⁵⁰The lord of that servant shall come in a day when he looketh not for him, and in an hour that he is not aware of, ⁵¹And shall cut him asunder, and appoint him his portion with the hypocrites: there shall be weeping and gnashing of teeth.

Mark 13:32-37 - ³²But of that day and that hour knoweth no man, no, not the angels which are in heaven, neither the Son, but the Father. ³³Take ye heed, watch and pray: for ye know not when the time is. ³⁴For the Son of man is as a man taking a far journey, who left his house, and gave authority to his servants, and to every man his work, and commanded the porter to watch. ³⁵Watch ye therefore: for ye know not when the master of the house cometh, at even, or at midnight, or at the cockcrowing, or in the morning: ³⁶Lest coming suddenly he find you sleeping. ³⁷And what I say unto you I say unto all, Watch.

These two passages comprise the primary Scriptural foundation for the doctrine of the "imminent return of Christ." The Lord is clearly communicating to the Church the need for vigilant preparedness lest she be caught off guard by His return. The command, ***Watch,*** is the preeminent imperative of these texts. In the contexts of these passages many signs of His return are given. The Church is accountable to ***watch*** for those signs lest she, in hapless self-indulgence, be caught off guard and be abruptly awakened by her Lord's return. The parable of the ten virgins[a] dramatically enforces this command to preparedness.

Yet the distinct teaching of these texts is not that Christ is coming without warning. Quite the contrary, these texts declare that the Lord will send many signs and warnings which His servants are directed to

---

a See Matthew 25:1-13.

be watching for. Jesus warns that His coming will surprise only those who are lazy, heedless, and who neglect to watch. To extract out of these passages a dogma that denies preceding signs of necessity negates the meaning of Christ's warnings and eliminates the ability to watch. If there is nothing to watch for then we cannot watch.

Notice also that these texts describe the bodily return of Jesus Christ, involving the damnation of the unrighteous and unprepared. Since both tribulational viewpoints agree that the damnation of the unrighteous occurs at Christ's return after the Tribulation,[a] these texts cannot be used to argue for an unannounced pretribulation Rapture of the Church. The focus of these "imminent return texts" is a warning to the righteous to be prepared for Jesus Christ's return to earth.

Please do not miss this cardinal point. Many pretribulationists want to say that the Rapture must be imminent (read: *must happen suddenly and without warning*,) but the physical return of Christ will be preceded by clear signs. Then they will use passages such as these to defend this contention. Yet these passages are expressly referring to the physical return of Christ to earth. Do you see the exegetical problem here? Texts of Scripture where pretribulationists find the terminology to argue for their imminent Rapture theory are expressly seen to be texts that are declaring Christ's bodily return to earth, but they do not consider Christ's bodily return to be imminent! There is unsound exegesis here. Claiming that the removal of the Church must be imminent or happen without warning in distinction to Christ's bodily return (which is not imminent because it will be preceded by clear signs,) and then using as authority for this "imminence" claim the terminology of texts that are explicitly referring to Christ's bodily return, is very shoddy exegesis! Texts that are clearly pointing to Christ's bodily return to earth direct His Church to watch lest she be caught unawares.

Therefore, if there is to be an imminent return of Christ than this return must include both the Rapture and His bodily return. From these texts we must affirm either that both events are imminent or neither are imminent. Further, any teaching that denies that signs will precede Christ's return to earth or the Rapture of the Church, is also at odds with these same "imminent return texts."

---

a See Matthew 24:30.

Statements like, *ye know not what hour your Lord doth come,*[a] and, *ye know not when the time is,*[b] should also be examined. To some these statements imply that no signs can precede Christ's return. I believe this to be an unnecessary assumption. Christ HAS NOT given to the Church the specific time of His coming (i.e. 10 years from His ascension, 100 years, 1000 years, etc.). That information could certainly cause large percentages of succeeding generations of Christians to grow lax. By now faith in Christ could very well have foundered on earth. Instead, God has left the Church with a sense of nearness and anticipation. He does this so she will be always on her guard watching for the signs. Since the hour of His coming is unknown, the Church must continually watch for the signs of her Lord's return! Christ has not revealed the day or hour of His return, but He has given the Church many signs which she is directed to watch for.

Revelation 3:11 - Behold, I come quickly: hold that fast which thou hast, that no man take thy crown.

Revelation 16:15 - Behold, I come as a thief. Blessed is he that watcheth, and keepeth his garments, lest he walk naked, and they see his shame.

Revelation 22:7 - Behold, I come quickly: blessed is he that keepeth the sayings of the prophecy of this book.

Revelation 22:12 - And, behold, I come quickly; and my reward is with me, to give every man according as his work shall be.

In these texts Christ's bodily appearing is again the focus. Indeed, the last three references are given in a context that includes the consummation of all events surrounding our Lord's return. Christ is coming quickly to receive His bride, to avenge the faithful martyrs, to judge the unrighteous, to destroy the armies of the enemy, to set up His

---

a Matthew 24:42.

b Mark 13:33.

reign on earth, etc. The fundamental directive of these texts, as with the Olivet texts, is watchful readiness. (***Blessed is he that watcheth, and keepeth his garments, lest he walk naked, and they see his shame.***[a])

Teaching that there are no signs preceding the Rapture does not produce vigilance it produces a sense of false security and negligence. There is distinct warning that these passages declare, namely, <u>unprepared servants may miss the signs of Christ's return</u>! Though many pretribulationists display an interest in the deceptions, persecutions, and deprivations of the Great Tribulation, this interest could often be described as detached. For they feel they need not personally concern themselves with such things, because Christ Jesus will Rapture them out of the earth before the real trouble begins. This disassociation seems to annul a main admonition of these passages. Indeed, deception, persecution, and tribulation are often the very things that the faithful are warned to prepare for. These texts do not deny precursory signs, they affirm them, and warn the Church to vigilantly watch for them!

Further Observations on Imminence

When the "imminent return texts" of Scripture were written they could not have meant that Christ's return for the Church could occur at any moment and without warning. There were still several things that needed to take place first. Millard J. Erickson, in his book, <u>Contemporary Options in Eschatology</u>,[b] has listed several examples of things that the Scriptures declare would happen, but their occurrences were still outstanding at the time of the writing of Scripture. Some examples are, Peter had to grow old and die;[c] the gospel had to reach to the uttermost parts of the earth (***ye shall be witnesses unto me... unto the uttermost part of the earth***[d]); the Church had to grow from a ***grain***

---

a Revelation 16:15.

b See Millard J. Erickson's, <u>Contemporary Options in Eschatology</u>, pg. 175.

c See John 21:18-19.

d Acts 1:8.

of mustard seed to become a **great tree;**[a] the disciples had to be hated and persecuted in all the world;[b] the apostle Paul was given the general outline of his life including his death;[c] Jerusalem had to be destroyed;[d] and there would be **blindness in part...to Israel, until the fulness of the Gentiles be come in.**[e]

In my opinion, at least two of these "initial" signs have not yet been fulfilled. Yet, even assuming, as some do, that these initial signs all came to pass by the end of the first century or shortly thereafter, it still remains that the "imminent Rapture texts" did not mean that Christ could come at any moment when the texts were first written, for these things had not all come to pass yet when these "imminent" texts were first written. Therefore, if the passages did not mean that Christ could come at any moment when they were penned then the texts cannot be vested with that meaning at some later date. Dr. Erickson states it this way; *"...when the passages that urge the readers to watch and wait were written, they could not have required their early readers to believe in imminence. Certain events had to be fulfilled before Christ would come. But if these passages did not require their early readers to believe in the imminence of Christ's coming, they do not require us to believe it either."*[f] Scripture speaks of many things that must come to pass before the Lord returns. This reality must clarify any doctrine of an *imminent* return of Christ.

As noted in chapter one, the Apostle Paul gave two specific signs in 2 Thessalonians 2:1-3 that have yet to be fulfilled. The Gentile Christians in Thessalonica were directed to watch for the fulfillment of these specific signs. And they were given unequivocal instructions not to expect Christ's return for them until these signs had come to pass. The imperative of the Apostle's instruction was to look for the signs!

---

a Luke 13:19.

b See John 15:18-25.

c See Acts 9:15, 22:15, 23:11, 26:2, 27:24, & 2 Timothy 4:5*ff*.

d See Matthew 23:37-24:2.

e Romans 11:25.

f Millard J. Erickson, <u>Contemporary Options in Eschatology</u>, pg. 175.

Therefore, Christ will not return for His Church until these signs have come to pass. The signs are; one, a great apostasy from the one true faith must occur; and, two, the Antichrist must be revealed. It is notable that the Christian Church was instructed by the Apostle to the Gentiles to first watch for the fulfillment of specific signs before expecting Christ's return.

One final observation should be made. Though many signs are given in Scripture that are signals of the nearness of Christ's return, this does not mean that mankind in general, nor the Church in particular will recognize those signs and take heed. There is a specific warning that emerges from the "imminent return" passages; namely, there is a distinct possibility and, yes, likelihood that even many in the Church will miss the signs of His coming and thereby be caught unawares. The signs are sure, yet only those who are spiritually alert will discern them. In the Revelation 16:15 text, Christ implores the saints who are far into the Tribulation period that they need to continue to be watchful or they will be caught off guard by His coming.

The command, *Watch*, speaks of diligent godly works and spiritual alertness and readiness. Christians are to be ***those who by reason of use have their senses exercised to discern both good and evil.***[a] This spiritual preparedness and vigilant discernment is essential to the believer's readiness for Jesus Christ's return.

In summary, it is inappropriate to teach that there are no signs that will precede the Rapture of the Church. In reality the Lord has given the Church several signs to watch for. There can certainly be a legitimate debate among Christians as to the meaning of these signs. It is indeed even appropriate to examine whether all the signs have come to pass. But to teach believers that it is wrong to watch for signs is itself Scripturally wrong and also dangerous. Any such teaching will most assuredly cause some believers to turn from Christ's command to vigilance and, thereby, miss the signs of Christ's soon return.

---

a Hebrews 5:14.

11:   The Church and Redeemed Israel

Perhaps the most distinct difference of understanding (outside of the timing of the Rapture itself) between pre and posttribulationism, is the respective differences of understanding of the relationship between believing Israel of the last days and the Christian Church. Generally speaking, pretribulationists make a marked distinction between the redeemed Israelites of the last days and the Christian Church. Some go so far as to say that redeemed Israel is the wife of Jehovah, whereas the Church is the bride of Christ.[a]

Most pretribulationists teach that after the Rapture of the Church, the Jewish people will finally realize that they rejected their Messiah at His first coming and will, at long last, turn to Him. This, they usually proclaim, will occur under a different dispensation.[b] By making this differentiation between the Church and redeemed Israel, considering the two to be separate redemptive bodies, pretribulationists claim license to teach that much of the Old and New Testament prophetic writings dealing with the time of the second coming of Christ are not applicable to the Christian Church, but only to redeemed Israel. For instance, the Olivet Discourse[c] is considered by many pretribulationists to describe only what redeemed Israel (and other Gentile converts in that "dispensation") will encounter after the Rapture of the Church and before the return of Christ. Pretribulationists teach that the "elect" of these texts are redeemed Israelites who are not part of the Christian Church. Jesus, they point out, was speaking to Israelites in this discourse and not to Christians (i.e. the disciples were all Jews). Many

---

a I heard the distinguished Dr. J. Vernon Magee use this description to differentiate between the Church and redeemed Israel. Though Dr. Magee is held in very high esteem by me, I cannot accept that this bigamous allegory is a proper depiction of God's relationship to the redeemed.

b Dispensationists teach that the world is now under the "dispensation of grace," during the Great Tribulation it will be under the "dispensation of wrath." Dispensationism is the underlying hermeneutic of most pretribulationists. It will not be extensively critiqued in this volume, but I reject the tenants of dispensationism, and consider this viewpoint unbiblical.

c Recorded in Matthew 24-25, Mark 13, & Luke 21.

Old Testament prophetic writings such as many of those found in the books of Isaiah, Daniel, and Ezekiel are generally regarded by pretribulationists as not applying to the Christian Church, but only to redeemed Israel and other Tribulation saints.

Also the bulk of the Revelation is typically declared to be inapplicable to the Christian Church. Most dispensationists teach that chapters 4-19 are not dealing with anything that applies directly to the Christian Church. The Christian Church is seen by them to be in heaven with Christ during this time. And the redeemed individuals on earth mentioned in these chapters are declared by them to be "tribulation saints"[a] and are distinct from the Church. They teach that the narrative only describes what those saints will endure on earth.

Since this hermeneutic of dispensationists has such far reaching implications; since it results in pretribulationism dividing the end times texts of Scripture, and saying that many of them do not apply to Christians, it is appropriate, yes, even imperative, that we examine it.

ISRAEL IN THE NEW TESTAMENT ECONOMY

The Jewish people, as physical descendants of Abraham through Isaac and Israel (Jacob) <u>ARE</u> the chosen people of God. Israelites were chosen of God to deliver to mankind the Word of God (***the oracles of God,***[b]) and chosen to be the special people who would bring forth the Messiah to mankind. Abraham, Isaac, and Israel (Jacob) and the physical children of Israel (Jacob) are the special people with whom God set up redemptive covenant relationship with. God blessed the Israelites by working out His great plan of redemption for mankind through them. The Israelites were of old and <u>ARE</u> today the chosen people of God. It is particularly important that Christians understand that the Israelites (Jews) of today are still God's chosen people. This is

---

a Pretribulationists teach the "tribulation saints" are chiefly redeemed Israelites, but they teach that this term also applies to an innumerable host of Gentile converts who have been led to Christ by redeemed Jews.

b Romans 3:2.

categorically declared to be the case by the Apostle Paul in Romans 11. He proclaims this reality by noting that *the gifts and calling of God are without repentance.*[a] Detestable prejudices and persecutions against the Jews abounded in the Middle Ages partly because Christians failed to understand that the Jews are still God's chosen people. Sadly, this error and the consequent abuses have continued right up to today.

This election of Israel by God, however, does not afford the Israelites any special means of redemption. They must, each one, trust in their Messiah the Lord Jesus Christ for the remission of their sins in order to be saved. Remission of sins and atonement comes only by the shed blood of the Lord Jesus Christ. As one Jewish apostle put it, *Neither is there salvation in any other: for there is none other name under heaven given among men, whereby we must be saved.*[b] Though this orthodoxy should be well understood by all Christians, a staggering number of Christians believe that somehow even unsaved Jewish people, though rejecting Jesus Christ as their Messiah, are in a special sanctioned place in God's redemptive economy. This is simply not so!

Several passages in the New Testament deal with issues related to the Children of Israel. These passages reveal many things about the chosen people. We understand, by these passages, that most of the Jews rejected their Messiah, the Lord Jesus, when He came unto them.[c] Further, that unbelieving Jews will be provoked to jealousy by Gentiles who believe in Christ Jesus and are blessed by Him.[d] Also, the host of Israel will one day finally realize their unbelief and turn to Christ.[e] The Scriptures also make it clear that God has preserved a remnant of believing Jews throughout redemptive history.[f]

Much of the book of Romans is devoted to defining Israel's place in God's great redemption plan. Beginning in chapter nine but

---

a Romans 11:29.

b Acts 4:12.

c See John 1:11.

d See Romans 10:19, 11:11, 14.

e See Romans 11:26.

f See Romans 9:27, 11:5.

particularly in chapter eleven the Apostle Paul explains that his *brethren* and *kinsmen according to the flesh*[a] (the Jews,) though being *natural branches*[b] in God's *olive tree,*[c] *were broken off*[d] God's olive tree because they rejected their Messiah. Thus, Israel has been *broken off because of unbelief,*[e] and Gentile believers, being from a *wild olive tree,*[f] have been grafted into God's *olive tree* through faith in Jesus Christ.[g] This was done so that the purposes of God might be accomplished in offering salvation to all men.

In the Church of Jesus Christ the prophecy of Hosea is fulfilled; *...I will have mercy upon her that had not obtained mercy; and I will say to them which were not my people, Thou art my people; and they shall say, Thou art my God.*[h] The New Testament fulfillment account of Hosea's prophecy proclaims, *...I will call them my people, which were not my people; and her beloved, which was not beloved. And it shall come to pass, that in the place where it was said unto them, Ye are not my people; there shall they be called the children of the living God.*[i]

Notice however, that there was no new olive tree set up. Through unbelief the majority of Israel was broken off (cut out of the Church), and, through belief, Gentiles were grafted in (made part of the Church). It is the same *good olive tree.*[j] This *good olive tree* is God's unitary redemptive body on earth and is by definition the Church!

It should also be noted that the majority of Israel will someday turn to Christ Jesus and be saved.[k] However, God will not come up with

---

a Romans 9:3.

b Romans 11:21, 24.

c Romans 11:17, 24.

d Romans 11:17, 20, 24.

e Romans 11:20.

f Romans 11:17.

g See Romans 11:20.

h Hosea 2:23.

i Romans 9:25-26.

j Romans 11:24.

k See Romans 11:26.

some new or modified plan of redemption, but rather, the eyes of Israel will one day be opened and they will turn to their Redeemer. In fact, the Bible even warns Gentile converts at this point: ***Boast not against the [cut out] branches... if God spared not the natural branches, take heed lest he also spare not thee.***[a] Rather than rejecting the Jews for their unbelief in the Messiah the Church should seek to evangelize physical Israelites. Christians should long for this restoration of the unbelieving Jews into the Church for that occurrence will identify a time of great blessedness on earth.

The Bible reveals that when revival begins in the house of Israel a glorious and hallowed day will have dawned. Concerning that glorious time and sign of the end days, the Bible states, ***I say then, Have they stumbled that they should fall? God forbid: but rather through their fall salvation is come unto the Gentiles, for to provoke them to jealousy. Now if the fall of them be the riches of the world, and the diminishing of them the riches of the Gentiles; how much more their fulness? ...For if the casting away of them be the reconciling of the world, what shall the receiving of them be, but life from the dead?***[b]

All the apostles and first disciples of the Lord, indeed most of the first Christians were Jewish. These Jews formed the foundation of the New Testament Church. There have been many Jews from then until now who have come to saving faith in the Lord Jesus Christ. These physical members of Israel who have believed on their Messiah are not separate from the Church, and none of their future believing kinsmen will be separated either! The Bible affirms quite distinctly, ***I say then, Hath God cast away his people? God forbid. For I also am an Israelite, of the seed of Abraham, of the tribe of Benjamin.***[c] The apostle went on to explain that God has preserved a remnant of believing Jews. A remnant that have come to saving faith in the Lord Jesus Christ. The Scripture states, ***at this present time also there is a***

a See Romans 11:18, 21

b Romans 11:11-12, 15.

c Romans 11:1.

remnant according to the election of grace. And if by grace, then is it no more of works: otherwise grace is no more grace... What then? Israel hath not obtained that which he seeketh for; but the election hath obtained it, and the rest were blinded.[a] This remnant is still attached to God's olive tree, and believing Gentiles which were from *a wild olive tree, wert graffed in among them, and with them partakest of the root and fatness of the olive tree.*[b]

We must understand though that there is no class system or dualism in God's redemption plan. All believing Jews are part of the Church. In fact the Bible makes it quite clear that all the redeemed throughout all human history are part of the Church. Moses is part of the Church.[c] Indeed, Abraham is part of the Church, and the father of faith.[d] Properly speaking, being a Christian (whether Jew or Gentile) makes a person a child of Abraham,[e] not physically but spiritually. Indeed the household of faith includes all the Old Testament saints. All the redeemed from Adam forward have been redeemed by the blood of the Lamb! Jesus, remember, is *the Lamb slain from the foundation of the world.*[f] Every redeemed individual that ever has or ever will enter into heaven will do so solely upon the merits of Jesus Christ's redemption. There is no one that has earned salvation or has acquired it in any other way! Truly, there is no other way to obtain salvation!

It is clear that God did not destroy or turn away from the *good olive tree* due to the unbelief of His own people. He cut out branches that were unfruitful and grafted in other branches that would produce good fruit. The *good olive tree*, or house of faith, or Church, is a single body. God does not have two redemption plans, one for Israelites and the other for Gentiles. There is a continuity and unity in the family of the redeemed, regardless of the ethnic stock of its members. It must be

---

a Romans 11:5-7.

b Romans 11:17.

c See Hebrews 11:23-28.

d See Romans 4:9-16 & Hebrews 11:7-10, 17-19.

e See Galatians 3:28-29.

f Revelation 13:8.

affirmed that there is no division in God's redemption plan for mankind. There is simply those who believe in Christ and those who do not. Those who believe have everlasting life, those who do not are on their way to everlasting damnation. (*He that believeth on him is not condemned: but he that believeth not is condemned already, because he hath not believed in the name of the only begotten Son of God.*[a])

Many other passages deal with the issue of Israel in the New Testament economy and one truth emerges from them all, namely, there is only one household of the faith (*good olive tree*) in God's redemptive plan. The Bible states clearly and emphatically, *There is neither Jew nor Greek, there is neither bond nor free, there is neither male nor female: for ye are all one in Christ Jesus. And if ye be Christ's, then are ye Abraham's seed, and heirs according to the promise.*[b]

I should again clearly emphasize that the real spiritual ethnic identity of the family of God (both Jews and Gentiles) is Jewish, or the seed of Abraham. This identity is not based upon a physical blood-line, it is based upon a spiritual blood-line (the blood of Christ). Jesus is *the Lion of the tribe of Juda, the Root of David.*[c] Therefore, those who are spiritually born again into Christ's family are descendants of Judah as well, not physically but spiritually.[d] Scripture states, *he is not a Jew, which is one outwardly; neither is that circumcision, which is outward in the flesh: But he is a Jew, which is one inwardly; and circumcision is that of the heart, in the spirit, and not in the letter; whose praise is not of men, but of God.*[e]

Therefore, the Gentile Church is not separate from redeemed Israel, it is part of redeemed Israel! If you believe in the Lord Jesus Christ

---

a John 3:18.

b Galatians 3:28-29.

c Revelation 5:5.

d Please note, this reality in no way negates the fact that physical Jews are God's chosen people. God has sternly warned all men against harming or even maligning His chosen people (physical Jews). A heresy, sadly prevalent in Christian Churches, that rejects the chosen status of the physical Jews of today is nothing less than a lie from hell!

e Romans 2:28-29.

then are ye Abraham's seed, and heirs according to the promise.[a]
Gentile Christians should always remember, however, that our spiritual
inclusion in the household of Israel, by faith in Jesus Christ, has not
eliminated the heritage of natural Israelites! The Apostle Paul explained
the special place of unbelieving physical Israelites in this way: *As
concerning the gospel, they are enemies for your sakes: but as
touching the election, they are beloved for the fathers' sakes.*[b] The
fathers referenced here are the patriarchs, Abraham, Isaac, Israel, and
the twelve son's of Israel.

With all these clear texts before us which deal with the place of the
Chosen People in God's economy, it should be clear that God has not
constructed a dualism in His redemption plan.   Therefore, it is
Scripturally unjustified and very dangerous to establish arbitrary
redemptive divisions in God's Word. If any particular passage does not
apply to the Christian Church the text itself will say so. When there is
no textual reason, then the text cannot be divided at random to appease
some particular theological viewpoint.   Simply put, if the texts in
question give no authority to the Bible student to exclude their
applicability, then such license must not be taken! Frightening heresies
will be the result of allowing arbitrary divisions in the Biblical texts.

All true Christians disdain the twisting and cutting up of Scripture
employed by cults and other false teachers. Yet, it is a slippery slope to
just that kind of corruption if we give our doctrinal preferences
precedent over the Biblical text. If I can say that Matthew 24 does not
apply to Gentile believers, because Jesus was speaking to only Jewish
disciples, then what is to stop me from saying that same thing about any
or all the other places in the Gospels where Jesus' audience is only
Jewish disciples?! This, then, is a subjective standard of interpretation.
It will, of necessity, produce error and heresy. The plain statements of
Scripture must be our authority, and must dictate our doctrinal
viewpoints. Human opinion is placed in authority above Holy Writ if
this order is reversed!!

---

a Galatians 3:29.

b Romans 11:28.

12:   Excluding the Olivet Discourse

Though dispensationists teach that many prophetic texts *"do not apply to the Church,"* it is imperative to specifically address their teaching that the Olivet Discourse does not apply to the Christian Church. The sermon that the Lord Jesus delivered to His disciples, recorded in Matthew 24-25, Mark 13, and Luke 21, is known as the *"Olivet Discourse."* Jesus was alone with His disciples on the Mount of Olives and He revealed to them in great detail many of the specifics of the last days and of His return. These passages give the clearest specific time line in Scripture regarding the return of Christ. Jesus lovingly furnished for His disciples a very precise time line of the events surrounding His second coming, and revealed many signs which will herald His return.

Pretribulationist doctrine typically declares that these texts apply only to the Tribulation saints. Tribulation saints are understood by them to be distinct from the Church and include Israelites who have finally accepted Jesus Christ and Gentiles who have been proselytized by these redeemed Jews. Where does such a belief come from? The Lord does not say or even imply anything in these passages to lead to such a conclusion. Actually, dispensationists do not claim authority for this teaching from the excluded texts themselves. Their authority to teach the inapplicability of such passages emerges from their overview belief that God has divided redemptive history into a series of distinct dispensations. The scriptures that are for one dispensation are often understood by them to not apply to other dispensations. Simply put, since their dispensational structure holds that the Tribulation period is in a different dispensation than the Church dispensation, then the texts that describe life on earth during the Tribulation do not apply to the Church.

Pretribulationists, however, will often try to find textual authority for this hermeneutic either in the words or setting of the excluded texts. I have heard some explain their belief that the Olivet Discourse does not apply to the Church by stating that at the time of the Olivet Discourse Christ's Jewish disciples had no way of even imagining the "Gentile Church Age." Therefore, Jesus was answering the disciples' questions in a way that would relate to the Jewish people. But does this explanation hold up to a Scriptural examination? Absolutely not!

It is clear that in the Olivet Discourse Jesus is speaking to his disciples as a representative body. Both pretribulationists and posttribulationists are in agreement on that point. Neither camp believes that all the things that are prophesied in this discourse happened personally to the disciples or in the days of the original disciples. The difference of opinion rests on what redemptive body the disciples represent.

Pretribulationists typically teach that the disciples represent Jews who rejected the Messiah and, after the Rapture of the Church, finally realize their mistake and exercise faith in the Lord Jesus Christ. Though, doubtless, they would not state it in that way or in so many words. Nonetheless, by their teaching that the disciples represent "tribulation saints" in distinction from the Christian Church, pretribulationists teach that the original disciples represented the apostate majority of the Israelites of their day, not the believing remnant.

Posttribulation doctrine proclaims, however, that the disciples represent those who have believed in Jesus Christ and are born again into the family of God. The disciples are members and the very pillars of the Church of God. They represent the Church of Jesus Christ, both Jew and Gentile. They are the faithful remnant of Israel who will take part in the Rapture. Indeed, as noted, the apostles are the very foundation pillars of the Church! (*Now therefore ye are no more strangers and foreigners, but fellowcitizens with the saints, and of the household of God; And are built upon the foundation of the apostles and prophets, Jesus Christ himself being the chief corner stone; In whom all the building fitly framed together groweth unto an holy temple in the Lord: In whom ye also are builded together for an habitation of God through the Spirit.[a])*

If there will be a pretribulation Rapture of the Church, then why did the Lord say that these various things would happen to the disciples? The disciples will take part in the Rapture! They cannot represent a group of people who will not take part in the Rapture. Perhaps the best way to discern the correct understanding of who the disciples are representing is to consider how the events of this prophecy would have affected the disciples had Christ returned in their lifetime.

In a first century AD pretribulation Rapture scenario all the disciples would have been raptured to heaven before most of the things would occur that Jesus warned them about, for the disciples were Christian believers. They would not be present on earth during the Tribulation period!! When the abomination of desolation occurred (the middle of the seventieth week of Daniel's prophecy, i.e. the middle of the Tribulation period) they would have already been raptured! So why, then, does Jesus say, ***When ye therefore shall see...[b]***? Jesus, speaking exclusively to His disciples, said, ***pray ye that your flight[c]*** from the Antichrist's attack will not occur in the winter nor on the Sabbath. But the disciples would have already been raptured to heaven in a pretribulation Rapture scenario and would have no need to make such prayers. From what menace would they need to flee while they worshipped around the throne in the heavenly kingdom?

In a first century AD pretribulation Rapture scenario it is obvious that the disciples cannot represent Israelites that accept Christ after a pretribulation Rapture, for the disciples would take part in the Rapture. To be a representative of a situation requires, of necessity, that the situation be able to apply to you personally. If a pretribulation Rapture of the Church is the premise, then the situation Jesus is speaking of in

---

a Ephesians 2:19-22.

b Matthew 24:15.

c Matthew 24:20.

the Olivet Discourse could never personally apply to His disciples. Regardless of the ethnic stock of the disciples they are part of the Church of Jesus Christ, and as such will take part in the Rapture of the Church!! If Christ had returned in their lifetime they would have taken part in the Rapture as living saints. Since they have already fallen asleep they will take part in the Rapture as resurrected saints. Either way the original disciples will take part in the Rapture! Therefore, the disciples cannot represent a group of people who come to Christ after a pretribulation Rapture under some different dispensation.

Do you see the problem? Jesus is clearly referring to these events as events that apply to His Christian disciples (either personally or as representatives), but they could not personally apply to His disciples in a pretribulation Rapture scenario. If Jesus was referring to the unbelieving majority of Israel here He would have assuredly said so. Instead of saying things like, **when ye therefore shall see...,**[a] and **pray ye that your flight...,**[b] and **if any man shall say unto you...,**[c] would He not have said things like, *When your unbelieving kinsmen shall see...,* or *pray for your relatives who have rejected me that their flight...,* or *tell your brethren that if any man shall say...,* etc.?

However, in a first century AD posttribulation Rapture scenario all of these admonitions of Christ make perfect sense. Christ is talking to His faithful disciples in this discourse. They are not unbelieving Jews, but believing Jews! They are not apostate Jews, they are faithful Jews! They are not separate from the Church, they are the very foundation pillars of the Church. Therefore Christ clearly intended for His disciples to understand that His Church, or **the elect,**[d] will still be on earth at the time of the end and will go through the Great Tribulation. Jesus used the second person plural pronouns *ye*, *you*, and *your* in speaking to His disciples twelve times in Matthew 24:4-28, twenty-two

---

a Matthew 24.15.

b Matthew 24:20.

c Matthew 24:23.

d Matthew 24:22.

times in Mark 13:7-29, and nineteen times in Luke 21:8-26. Each of these sections are specifically referring to the time of the Great Tribulation. He clearly intended to declare that the Tribulation events which He was describing applied to His disciples. If Christ Jesus had returned in the first century, then those first disciples would have gone through the Great Tribulation.

If Christ's original disciples were the elect of the Olivet Discourse, then Christ's disciples of the last days are also the elect of this discourse. There is no other way around this issue. It is a cardinal truth that must be received! Jesus taught the original Church leaders that He would continue to build His Church and, in the latter days, His Church would endure the Great Tribulation! It is offensive to teach that these great words of her Lord and Master do not apply to her! It will also engender heresy to teach such things!

It should also be noted that Jesus spoke of a Rapture of believers in the Olivet Discourse. But He emphatically stated that it would occur at His return and ***Immediately after the tribulation of those days***![a] Please do not miss this crucial point. In the Olivet Discourse Jesus revealed: (1) that an unprecedented time of Great Tribulation is coming upon the earth;[b] (2) that immediately after that Great Tribulation He will appear in the clouds of heaven on His return journey to earth;[c] and, (3) that as He is coming in the clouds, a trumpet will sound and Christ will send His angles to gather His elect in the air.[d] This is a precise time line and plainly reveals that the Rapture will occur after the Great Tribulation. Is it any wonder that those who reject this time line must also reject the applicability of the texts that declare it?

There is no place in Scripture where the pretribulationist can turn to that specifically unfolds a time line to support his view of a pretribulation Rapture. No such text with a pretribulation Rapture time

---

a Matthew 24:29.

b See Matthew 24:21, Mark 13:19, & Luke 21:22.

c See Matthew 24:29-30, Mark 13:24-26, & Luke 21:27.

d See Matthew 24:31 & Mark 13:27.

line exists. The reader is challenged here, find a passage that declares that there will be a Rapture of the Church, then the Great Tribulation, and then the bodily return of Christ. I assure you that you will not find any such passage anywhere in Holy Writ, for no such passage exists in the Scriptures.

It is truly troubling that some pretribulationists feel compelled to cut out the Olivet Discourse and say it does not apply to the Christian Church. It seems that since they do not believe in a posttribulation Rapture of the Church, and since the Olivet Discourse directly outlines just that, a decision has been made to simply avoid the trouble the Olivet Discourse causes for their doctrinal position by declaring an inapplicability of these texts. Yet this cannot be allowed! Scripture dictates doctrine not the reverse. Doctrine is, therefore, wholly subservient to Scripture!

13:   The Secret Rapture Theory

There is a commonly held belief in the Church today that there will be a sudden disappearance of Christians all over the earth, happening in a moment of time, and occurring without warning or explanation. But this teaching of a sudden and secretive disappearance of the Church from the earth, to her surprise, leaving the rest of the inhabitants of the world dumbfounded and searching for answers, seems to be a doctrine strange to Scripture.

1 Thessalonians 4:15-17 is perhaps the most well known and clearest passage in all of Scripture specifically describing the Rapture of the Church. In this passage we learn that there will be three specific and loud harbingers of the Lord's coming. The text states that *the Lord himself shall descend from heaven with a shout, with the voice of the archangel, and with the trump of God.*[a]

It seems quite obvious from this text that Jesus is not intending to receive His Church unto Himself secretly. This threefold reference to profound and audible heralds of Christ's return suggests a strong intent to be noticed. He will not merely come for His bride, He will come with a *shout.* In Revelation 1, when John the Apostle saw the risen Lord, he reported that the Lord's voice was *as the sound of many waters.*[b] The Lord's shout, therefore, must be deafening! Certainly the archangel's voice is thunderous, and it is hard to believe that the sound of the *trump of God* could be anything less than resounding. Furthermore, Revelation 1 also reveals that *every eye shall see him* when *he cometh with clouds.*[c] The texts of Scripture that describe the Rapture of the Church argue against secrecy or stealth, they in no way support it.

It seems odd then that this supposed mysterious disappearance of millions of people all over the world, including every child under the

---

a 1 Thessalonians 4:16.

b Revelation 1:15.

c Revelation 1:7.

age of accountability and every child in his mother's womb, is not once mentioned in Scripture? From the perspective of the "left-behind" world this would be the single greatest catastrophe in history after the Noahic flood. Presumably, parents would be in abject despair and would wander the earth in search of their children. Every unbelieving expectant mother would suddenly discover that the child within her is gone. This would be the greatest witness to the left-behind world that Christ's claims are true. Why then does not the Bible ever describe such an event? Several hundred years before it occurred, God's prophets prophesied that the women of Judea would suffer the desolation of seeing their children murdered before their eyes.[a] That was a horrible event, but it was confined to the region of Judea under Herod's rule. This loss of children would be worldwide. The scope of such an event is unimaginable.

Assuredly this sudden disappearance would cause global horror and remorse to a degree that has never been known before, so why haven't the prophets foretold of it? The Rapture is mentioned several times, but a mysterious disappearance of the Church of Jesus Christ (and all children under the age of accountability) while a puzzled rest of the world continues along trying to figure out what happened is not once mentioned. An event of such world shaking magnitude would most certainly have been mentioned, and mentioned often in Scripture.

Some may object by asking, *"Will not the Rapture involve this strange and inexplicable disappearance whether it happens before or after the Tribulation?"* The answer to this query is an emphatic, NO! The Rapture spoken of in the Bible is an event that happens at the very coming of the Lord. Every eye shall see Christ returning. While He is returning to earth, the redeemed (including those under the age of accountability and children in the womb) will be raptured up to meet Him. Those who are not raptured shall wail because of him.[b] There will be no confusion on anybody's part as to what is happening. This

---

a See Jeremiah 31:15 & Matthew 2:17-18.

b See Revelation 1:7.

will be the end of the world as it is known, and the beginning of Christ's millennial kingdom.

Often, pretribulationists teach that after the Rapture the Antichrist will claim that invaders from space or some other earth threatening menace is responsible for this massive and worldwide disappearance of people. The evil one, they say, will point to this "catastrophe" as incentive for the world to unify behind him. Yet, would not God leave abundant witness in His Word declaring that He is responsible? It is inconceivable that Holy Writ would remain silent about an event of such magnitude.

There are two references that deserve examination at this point. These two passages describe a *"taking away"* incident that will occur at the ***coming of the Son of man.*** The Matthew text specifically sets the timing of this event to be ***Immediately after the tribulation of those days.***[a]

Matthew 24:36-41 - [36]*But of that day and hour knoweth no man, no, not the angels of heaven, but my Father only.* [37]*But as the days of Noe were, so shall also the coming of the Son of man be.* [38]*For as in the days that were before the flood they were eating and drinking, marrying and giving in marriage, until the day that Noe entered into the ark,* [39]*And knew not until the flood came, and took them all away; so shall also the coming of the Son of man be.* [40]*Then shall two be in the field; the one shall be taken, and the other left.* [41]*Two women shall be grinding at the mill; the one shall be taken, and the other left.*

Luke 17: 26-37 - [26]*And as it was in the days of Noe, so shall it be also in the days of the Son of man.* [27]*They did eat, they drank, they married wives, they were given in marriage, until the day that Noe entered into the ark, and the flood came, and destroyed them all.*

---

a Matthew 24:29.

²⁸Likewise also as it was in the days of Lot; they did eat, they drank, they bought, they sold, they planted, they builded; ²⁹But the same day that Lot went out of Sodom it rained fire and brimstone from heaven, and destroyed them all. ³⁰Even thus shall it be in the day when the Son of man is revealed. ³¹In that day, he which shall be upon the housetop, and his stuff in the house, let him not come down to take it away: and he that is in the field, let him likewise not return back. ³²Remember Lot's wife. ³³Whosoever shall seek to save his life shall lose it; and whosoever shall lose his life shall preserve it. ³⁴I tell you, in that night there shall be two men in one bed; the one shall be taken, and the other shall be left. ³⁵Two women shall be grinding together; the one shall be taken, and the other left. ³⁶Two men shall be in the field; the one shall be taken, and the other left. ³⁷And they answered and said unto him, Where, Lord? And he said unto them, Wheresoever the body is, thither will the eagles be gathered together.

The first point that should be noted about these two texts is that there is a marked difference of opinion concerning what *taken* is referring to here. Some believe that *taken* refers to the Rapture of the Church. Others believe that *taken* refers to the wicked being delivered unto damnation. This difference of understanding is not defined to one Tribulation camp or the other. Many pretribulationist theologians believe that *taken* refers to judgment here and many other pretribulationist theologians believe that *taken* refers to the Rapture. The same can be said of posttribulationist theologians.

In Luke's account the disciples asked the Lord Jesus where these ones will be *taken*. Their question was, *"Where, Lord?"* In His answer the Lord employed the metaphor of eagles being gathered around a dead body. This answer from the Lord, and the fact that the focus in both Matthew and Luke is on those who have been taken in judgment in the past, makes the argument for being *taken in judgment* seem much more plausible. In these passages, the ones that have been *taken* in judgment include the people of Noah's generation who were all taken away by the flood, and the inhabitants of Sodom and Gomorrah in Lot's day who were destroyed by fire and brimstone from heaven. Jesus even soberly instructed His disciples to *"Remember Lot's wife."*

However, it may very well be that the *taken* ones here are the Christians being Raptured. Though this is an abrupt event as the Rapture will be, the context in no way says or implies that it is a secretive event. To the contrary, these passages describe a startling and dreadful event that will be in no way secretive or mysterious. Whether *taken* refers to judgment or Rapture, the event clearly involves the wicked falling into unexpected destruction, and the posttribulation viewpoint is consistent with this prophetic description of events surrounding Christ's return.

The events pictured here can be seen from two vantage points. At the Lord Jesus Christ's second coming the righteous will be *taken* up in the Rapture and the wicked will be *left* behind encountering God's wrath. Also at the second coming of Christ the wicked will be *taken* away in wrath and the righteous will be *left* to enjoy the millennial kingdom. Either way there will be no one wandering around trying to figure out what happened! And again, the timing of this event is established beyond question to be *Immediately after the tribulation of those days.*[a]

A further and perhaps more grave difficulty, however, with this secret Rapture teaching, is that this understanding seems to destroy a primary deception-detecting clue that Jesus left for His watchful disciples. This clue was given by Christ to aid in discerning false Christs and deception about His coming. The only place in the Bible where a supposed secretive coming of Christ is mentioned is in Matthew's gospel. However, in that passage the Lord Jesus Himself told His disciples not to believe in a secretive coming. *Behold if they shall say unto you, Behold, he is in the desert; go not forth: behold, he*

---

a Matthew 24:29.

is in the <u>secret</u> chambers; believe it not.[a] The Lord's instruction here is given for the particular purpose of teaching His followers how to battle deception. Christ Jesus gave some very distinct discernment counsel here. He stated, *if any man shall say unto you, Lo, here is Christ, or there; believe it not. For there shall arise false Christs, and false prophets, and shall show great signs and wonders; insomuch that, if it were possible, they shall deceive the very elect.*[b]

He then went on to tell His disciples that His return will be so obvious in the world that not only believers, but all people will know He has come. Jesus used two metaphors to teach His disciples that His coming would be an event obvious to all the world's population. He taught that just as a flash of lightening is obvious in a storm and as carrion birds circling in the air signal that a carcass is in sight, so His return would also be overtly obvious. (*For as the lightning cometh out of the east, and shineth even unto the west; so shall also the coming of the Son of man be. For wheresoever the carcase is, there will the eagles be gathered together.*[c]) The meaning of the Lord seems quite clear here. His coming for His disciples will be perceptible to all. *Every eye shall see him.*[d] No one will ask the question, "Is this Christ?" There will be no doubt on anyone's part. In fact, if anyone can ask, "Is this Christ?" be he believer or unbeliever, then it assuredly will not be Christ. Neither the righteous nor the wicked will be confused in that hour. The righteous will be raptured into His presence, the wicked will wail and mourn and cry out for the rocks to fall on them to hide them from His face, and the ignorant and undecided will behold in wonder and awe. No one will be left in doubt!

Jesus taught His disciples that in the midst of great deception there is one sure way they can know it is Him when He comes. That way? His coming will not be secretive! It will be loud and obvious to the whole world. Do not overlook the fact that the reference here is the

---

a Matthew 24:26.

b Matthew 24:23-24.

c Matthew 24:27-28.

d Revelation 1:7.

coming for His disciples. Since Christians are Christ's disciples they must realize that His coming for them will not be silent or secretive. This will be His Triumphal Entry. The Word of God powerfully proclaims, *it is written, As I live, saith the Lord, every knee shall bow to me, and every tongue shall confess to God.*[a] Paul presented this powerful proclamation to remind Christians that the coronation of Christ will be witnessed by all men, but especially by them.

In summary, it seems that the Lord's instruction to His Church on this matter is quite emphatic. Any teaching that advances a secretive return of Christ is not to be believed. Therefore, Christians who would follow Christ's instruction must make this clear proclamation. Christ is not going to return for His Church secretly! Christian, do not follow any teaching that says otherwise!

---

a Romans 14:11.

14:   The "Mystery Doctrine" Defense

As was noted earlier, from cover to cover, the Bible does not contain any one passage that unfolds a pretribulation Rapture time line. In the face of this and other textual problems with their doctrinal viewpoint, an argument commonly used by some pretribulationists to defend their position is that the pretribulation Rapture is a "mystery doctrine." They mean by this designation that God has kept the Rapture of the Church under a shroud of mystery in Scripture.

It seems that this defense is often used to skirt a pertinent textual discussion where the pretribulation view is wanting. I have personally experienced the use of this defense by many pretribulationists on several occasions. Therefore, this somewhat clandestine teaching of many pretribulationists should be brought out into the light for an open Scriptural examination. This, as well as all Christian teachings, must stand the test of the Word of God or be rejected.

There are indeed many "mystery doctrines" in the Bible. A non-exhaustive list includes, *the blindness of Israel,*[a] *the wisdom of God,*[b] *the glorification of the redeemed,*[c] *God's will,*[d] *the redemption plan of God, specifically, the inclusion of the Gentiles,*[e] *the relationship of Christ and His Church,*[f] *the gospel,*[g] *the working of iniquity in the world,*[h] and *saving faith in God.*[i]

By these many specific uses of the word *mystery*, the Biblical use of the word is well established. Without exception, the use of *mystery* in Scripture refers to a doctrine that could never be understood or

---

a See Romans 11:25.

b See 1 Corinthians 2:7.

c See 1 Corinthians 15:51.

d See Ephesians 1:9.

e See Ephesians 3:1-11 & Colossians 1:25-2:1; see also, Romans 16:25.

f See Ephesians 5:32.

g See Ephesians 6:19.

h See 2 Thessalonians 2:7.

i See 1 Timothy 3:9.

discerned by men without a special revelation from God. Most often *mystery* refers to an area of God's economy that requires Scriptural revelation to be understood, but it may also refer to an aspect of satanic working that requires Scriptural revelation.

Following are some examples of the Biblical use of *mystery*. God's whole plan of redemption is defined as a mystery: ***Now to him that is of power to stablish you according to my gospel, and the preaching of Jesus Christ, according to the revelation of the <u>mystery</u>, which was kept secret since the world began, But now is made manifest, and by the scriptures of the prophets, according to the commandment of the everlasting God, made known to all nations for the obedience of faith.***[a] It is doubtful that any Bible believing Christian assumes that *mystery* here means that the God's plan of redemption is unclear or shadowy in Scripture. The word, ***mystery,*** simply means that had God not revealed the said truth in His Word it could not have been figured out by men.

The incarnation, ministry, and ascension of Christ is a ***mystery*** doctrine. The Bible states, ***And without controversy great is the <u>mystery</u> of godliness: God was manifest in the flesh, justified in the Spirit, seen of angels, preached unto the Gentiles, believed on in the world, received up into glory.***[b] Even God's chosen people did not fully understand God's redemption plan. The reality that God would become a man and suffer and die for mankind's redemption, could not have been figured out by men. Therefore, God revealed this great truth to mankind in His Word. Yet, it is certain that there are many specific passages of Scripture that proclaim the incarnation of Christ. ***Mystery*** here does not mean that Christ's incarnation and redemptive ministry is shadowy or veiled in Scripture. Quite the contrary, it means that it takes the clear Scriptural revelation to understand it.

This must be clearly understood, ***mystery*** means simply that mankind, even God's own people, could not have figured out God's

a Romans 16:25-26.

b 1 Timothy 3:16.

working on their own. Therefore, God gave special Biblical revelation. Christian's can turn to numerous passages of Scripture that affirm the gospel plan. The Bible is replete with references to Christ's divinity. *Mystery* in Scripture does not mean that a teaching is murky or secretive, it only means that it would have been wholly unknown had God not revealed it to us in His Word. Actually, the Biblical doctrines that are *mystery* are generally the ones most explained in Scripture.

Nevertheless, some pretribulationists want to use the term, *mystery*, in an almost esoteric sense. It is as if they are saying that the pretribulational Rapture is not Scripturally revealed because it is a mystery. Therefore you must have some higher knowledge to discern it. This use of the term actually contradicts the Biblical usage. Some even come close to a Gnostic "higher knowledge" philosophy in their understanding of *mystery*. They do not have the plain statements of Scripture so they claim that some innate or Spirit delivered higher knowledge reveals to them that there will be a pretribulation Rapture.

This pretribulationist usage is an unbiblical usage of *mystery*. There is no place in Scripture where *mystery* means that the said doctrine is not revealed in God's Word. In every particular, **mystery** means that the doctrine is only revealed in God's word.

Therefore, if there is truly going to be a pretribulation Rapture of the Church, and if this pretribulation Rapture is a *"mystery doctrine,"* then the Bible student can expect to turn to several places in Scripture where this pretribulation Rapture *"mystery"* is unfolded. Ah, but here's the rub, Holy Writ does not spell out a pretribulation Rapture. As stated earlier, the only Scriptural time lines of the Rapture are all posttribulational!

The seeming purpose for the pretribulationist's use of this "mystery doctrine" argument is to project an air of authority presumably received by extra-Biblical discernment. He claims some special spiritual discernment has shown him that a pretribulation Rapture awaits the Church. If the rest of us can't see it, then we just aren't spiritual enough. This, however, is not a new tactic, but it is unusual to see

Bible-believing Christians use it! Cult leaders and other false teachers often use this method of indoctrination. They claim that they are the source of a secret higher knowledge and thereby deceive or intimidate their followers into accepting their teachings. There is a significant psychological power of coercion in this tactic.

However, the pretribulationists who use this "mystery doctrine argument" are true and Bible believing Christians. They would never allow the application of such mysticism or liberalism of interpretation to any other area of Scripture. On any other issue, this type of coercion and permissiveness of interpretation would be abhorrent to these pretribulationist brethren. For some reason, however, many fly fast and free on their Rapture doctrine.

Because many things related to the Lord's first and second comings are mysteries, it is sure that God has plainly and clearly revealed them in His Word. The Bible is now complete, man need not wait for any new revelations. Anything that God will reveal to man is contained within the 66 books of the Old and New Testaments. The Old Testament saints did not have the full Biblical revelation. New Testament saints, however, have all the Oracles of God. The fulness of time has come.

Any Christian doctrine must stand in the light of Scripture; if it cannot, then it must be wholly rejected! The doctrines of God are indeed spiritually discerned, and the Holy Spirit will only use the Word of God to teach them. Little children are able to understand God's truth. Jesus rejoiced in this fact; *In that hour Jesus rejoiced in spirit, and said, I thank thee, O Father, Lord of heaven and earth, that thou hast hid these things from the wise and prudent, and hast revealed them unto babes: even so, Father; for so it seemed good in thy sight.*[a]

There are many people who will study Scripture to find out the truth of God on other issues. Yet, when it comes to the end times and the Rapture of the Church they feel they cannot understand what God's Word has to say. On this subject they believe they must "defer to the

---

a Luke 10:21.

experts." God has assuredly commanded Christians to honor authority. He has raised up leaders in His Church, and holds all Christians accountable to show honor to these leaders and be under the authority structures He has established. However, Christians must realize that God has not raised up leaders in His Church so that they would study the Bible for everyone else. Rather, He has raised them up to admonish and equip all believers to study God's Word. It is the solemn duty of the leaders in the Church to be examples to all believers! God has also commanded all believers to examine and prove their teachers and leaders by the Word of God!

O for Berean Christians! Christians who will search the Scriptures daily to see if what they are being taught is so, even what they are taught about last things and the Rapture of the Church. Please realize, dear brother or sister, God will help you understand. If you pray in faith for wisdom God will give it, liberally and without upbraiding you.[a]

Also, please do not be intimidated by the so-called "experts." God has given His Word to the common man, and the common man who is filled with the Holy Spirit, and who diligently studies the Word of God, can discern God's meaning and understand it. Indeed, all Christians need to remember this humbling truth: ***God hath chosen the foolish things of the world to confound the wise; and God hath chosen the weak things of the world to confound the things which are mighty; And base things of the world, and things which are despised, hath God chosen, yea, and things which are not, to bring to nought things that are: That no flesh should glory in his presence. But of him are ye in Christ Jesus, who of God is made unto us wisdom, and righteousness, and sanctification, and redemption: That, according as it is written, He that glorieth, let him glory in the Lord.***[b]

Remember how surprised the leaders of Israel were when they examined the first Apostles? (***Now when they saw the boldness of Peter and John, and perceived that they were unlearned and ignorant***

---

a See James 1:5.

b 1 Corinthians 1:27-31.

men, they marvelled; and they took knowledge of them, that they had been with Jesus.[a]) This wonder of the leaders was based in the fact that they knew the Apostles to be unlearned. Yet they beheld their formidable ability to Scripturally defend their belief in Christ and to even persuade learned antagonists. This wisdom of the disciples was Spirit delivered. Christians serve the same God today. *For God, who commanded the light to shine out of darkness, hath shined in our hearts, to give the light of the knowledge of the glory of God in the face of Jesus Christ.*[b]

---

a Acts 4:13.

b 2 Corinthians 4:6.

15: Christ's Appearing

The word *appear* has a very specific meaning in God's Word. It means *to bring forth into the light, to come into view, to present one's self, to become visible, to manifest one's self.*[a] In the physical sense there is no doubt that the word means that someone or something is or becomes visible to the naked eye. The first two entries in Webster's dictionary on *appear* read as follows: *(1.) To come or be in sight; to be in view; to become visible. And God said, Let... the dry land appear. Gen. i. 9; (2.) To stand or attend in the presence of some authority, tribunal, or superior, to answer a charge, plead a cause, etc.; to present oneself as a party or advocate before a court, or as a person to be tried; to enter an appearance. We must all appear before the judgment seat. 2 Cor. v. 10.*[b]

There are 10 verses in the New Testament that define Christ's coming for His Church with the words ***appear*** or ***appearing***. Christ will be visible when He returns for the Church. This means that His return for the Church cannot take place in a split second as some claim. The human eye cannot see something that takes place that fast. The angels told the upward gazing disciples, ***Ye men of Galilee, why stand ye gazing up into heaven? this same Jesus, which is taken up from you into heaven, shall so come in like manner <u>as ye have seen him go into heaven.</u>***[c] Christ's first century disciples saw Him ascend out of their midst into heaven. Therefore, His last-days disciples shall see Him descend from heaven. Hallelujah!

It is at the time when the Lord Jesus Christ is actually seen in the clouds of glory by all men that the Church (risen and living) will be instantaneously ushered up into His presence. The Lord described this event with these words: ***And then shall appear the sign of the Son of man in heaven: and then shall all the tribes of the earth mourn, and***

---

a James Strong, <u>The Greek Dictionary of the NT</u>, 75(#5318-19) & various entries.

b <u>Webster's New International Dictionary</u>, pg. 129.

c Acts 1:11.

they shall see the Son of man coming in the clouds of heaven with power and great glory. And he shall send his angels with a great sound of a trumpet, and they shall gather together his elect from the four winds, from one end of heaven to the other.[a] Notice that the Scripture manifestly declares that first, all men shall see Him, and then the elect will be gathered unto Him. The Church shall see Him and rejoice, the wicked shall see Him and wail, but all men shall see Him! The Bible says, ***Behold, he cometh with clouds; and <u>every eye shall see him</u>, and they also which pierced him: and all kindreds of the earth shall wail because of him. Even so, Amen.***[b]

The Bible describes the first coming of the Lord Jesus Christ with the word *appearing*: ***But is now made manifest by the appearing of our Saviour Jesus Christ, who hath abolished death, and hath brought life and immortality to light through the gospel.***[c] Of a surety the first ***appearing*** of Christ was not momentary or capricious. It will be the same with His second ***appearing***, it will be open and evident to all.

The following texts all describe the second coming of Christ with the words *appear* or *appearing*. Notice that the setting up of His kingdom and the distribution of judgment is either explicit or implicit in each reference.

When Christ, who is our life, shall appear, then shall ye also appear with him in glory. (Colossians 3:4)

That thou keep this commandment without spot, unrebukeable, until the appearing of our Lord Jesus Christ: (1 Timothy 6:14)

I charge thee therefore before God, and the Lord Jesus Christ, who shall judge the quick and the dead at his appearing and his kingdom; (2 Timothy 4:1)

---

a Matthew 24:30-31.

b Revelation 1:7.

c 2 Timothy 1:10.

Henceforth there is laid up for me a crown of righteousness, which the Lord, the righteous judge, shall give me at that day: and not to me only, but unto all them also that love his appearing. (2 Timothy 4:8)

Looking for that blessed hope, and the glorious appearing of the great God and our Saviour Jesus Christ; (Titus 2:13)

So Christ was once offered to bear the sins of many; and unto them that look for him shall he appear the second time without sin unto salvation. (Hebrews 9:28)

That the trial of your faith, being much more precious than of gold that perisheth, though it be tried with fire, might be found unto praise and honour and glory at the appearing of Jesus Christ: (1 Peter 1:7)

And when the chief Shepherd shall appear, ye shall receive a crown of glory that fadeth not away. (1 Peter 5:4)

And now, little children, abide in him; that, when he shall appear, we may have confidence, and not be ashamed before him at his coming. (1 John 2:28)

Beloved, now are we the sons of God, and it doth not yet appear what we shall be: but we know that, when he shall appear, we shall be like him; for we shall see him as he is. (1 John 3:2)

Though there are some who would advance a theory that the Lord Jesus Christ's return for His church will be a startling and momentary event, those who hold such views receive no support from the Scriptural use of the word *appear*. These texts establish that the *appearing* of Christ referenced in the Word of God is not a momentary event. It can be positively affirmed that the event described in the preceding verses carries a permanence and finality to it that cannot but be understood as a crowning event of redemption.

The preceding verses also demonstrate how the Bible often uses the same word to describe all aspects of Christ's second advent. The Bible declares with parallel terminology that Christ will appear (come) for the Church and that Christ will appear (come) to set up His millennial kingdom on earth. This consistent usage of equivalent terminology declares that both of these two happenings are part of the same event. The Bible in no place divides the return, or coming, or appearing of Christ into two events. Indeed, there are many things that will take place when He appears (returns, comes), but His second coming will only happen once!

16: General Observations

IMPRUDENT TEACHINGS

In several particulars it can be seen that some who hold to a pretribulation Rapture viewpoint have a tendency to couple imprudent teachings with their eschatological viewpoint. The following bullet pointed list is an example of some of the indiscreet understandings that some pretribulationists hold. I have personally encountered the promotion of each of these ideas by various pretribulationist teachers. *[My comments are italicized in brackets]:*

- The Tribulation saints must pay for their salvation with their own blood. *[Brothers in Christ, the Church through the ages has identified any teaching that places any other sacrifice for sin over or alongside the blood sacrifice of Christ as the vilest heresy! Only the shed blood of Christ has redemptive merit. A fallen human's death has never had and will never have any redemptive merit whatsoever!]*

- During the Tribulation, God will partially revert back to the Old Testament law as a means of redemption. The references to the law in Revelation 12:17 and 14:12 are given as proofs of this. *[This again has been expressly identified in the Word of God, and by the Church of God, as grave heresy. The finished work of Christ is mankind's only hope of redemption! The book of Hebrews makes it quite clear that adherence to the law and the sacrificial system never has and never will save anyone. (**For the law having a shadow of good things to come, and not the very image of the things, can never with those sacrifices which they offered year by year continually make the comers thereunto perfect. For then would they not have ceased to be offered? because that the worshippers once purged should have had no more conscience of sins. But in those sacrifices there is a remembrance again made of sins every year. For*** *it is not possible that the blood of bulls and of goats should take away sins.*[a]*)   There can be no going back to the law, neither completely nor in part!!!]*

- During the Great Tribulation the Holy Spirit will have been removed from the earth, so the work of drawing people to the Lord will be assigned to the 144,000 Jewish evangelists. *[Again, any teaching that substitutes the convicting, convincing work of the Holy Spirit for some work of man has been identified by Christians through the ages as heresy! There can never be a time when fallen men are wooed to Christ by any other power but the holy power of the Holy Spirit!! He, alone, is able to draw men to salvation!]*

- The vengeance called for by the martyrs under the altar[b] is evidence that the Holy Spirit has been removed from earth, since there is no Christian forgiveness of enemies mentioned or called for. *[This theory is particularly amusing considering the fact that these martyrs are already in heaven when they pray this prayer. In reality, this prayer is a holy prayer, lifted to God by redeemed individuals who have been martyred by the Antichrist's wicked hordes. Please note that Scripture records God's holy answer to this prayer two chapters later.[c]]*

- Israel is the wife of Jehovah, whereas the Church is the Bride of Christ. *[God the Father, God the Son, and God the Holy Ghost, the Triune God is Jehovah! Are we then to understand that God is a polygamist?]*

- The Christian Church is not present on earth after chapter three of Revelation, the call to John from heaven, ***come up hither,***[d] being a euphemism for the Rapture of the Church. *[This is a claim that supports a doctrinal viewpoint, (i.e. the Church is in*

---

a Hebrews 10:1-4.

b Revelation 6:9.

c Revelation 8:1-5.

d Revelation 4:1.

heaven with Christ, having already been raptured) but is unsupported by Scripture. There are multiple references to redeemed individuals living on earth in chapters four through nineteen of Revelation.[a] Lacking any textual justification for this claim, its tenants should be rejected!]

THE CHURCH FATHERS AND THE REFORMATION FATHERS

A study of Church history will reveal that the dividing of Christ's return into two events (i.e. Christ returns *for* His Church, then, seven years later, He returns *with* His Church) is a very new doctrine. This belief emerged in the mid-nineteenth century. Prior to that it is not found among the doctrines of the Church. Since the time of the Church fathers the predominant belief of Christian theologians has been that Christ's return will be a singular event. At His return the wicked and the righteous will be separated **one from another, as a shepherd divideth his sheep from the goats.**[b]

Through the centuries believers have expected some very specific things to occur before the Lord's return. Historically, the general admonition to believers followed these points: Just before Christ's second coming the Antichrist will launch a hideous and vicious attack upon the Church. During this time of great trouble believers will be purified from earthly attachments and prepared to meet their Lord. This attack of the Antichrist will ultimately be foiled by the return of Christ, at which time the Antichrist and his evil cohorts will suffer the wrath of almighty God. This is the historic and consistent doctrinal position of the Church of Christ.

George E. Ladd, in his book, The Blessed Hope, states of the Church fathers:

Every church father who deals with the subject expects the church to suffer at the hands of Antichrist. God would purify

---

a A non-exhaustive list includes: Revelation 6:9-11, 7:3-14; 9:4, 11:3, 12:11, 14:1-12, 16:6; 18:4, 24, 20:4.

b Matthew 25:32.

the church through suffering, and Christ would save her by His return at the end of the Tribulation when He would destroy Antichrist, deliver His church, and bring the world to an end and inaugurate His millennial kingdom. The prevailing view is a posttribulation premillennialism.[a]

Virtually all the reformation fathers, including Martin Luther, John Calvin, and John Knox spoke and taught often on the subject of Christians facing the evils and tribulations of the Antichrist. Martin Luther, in particular, even taught that the pope was the Antichrist and the papal system was his evil ***mystery of iniquity.*** (Please note, I neither agree with, nor do I endorse this opinion of the papacy. Rather, this example is used to demonstrate the firm belief held by these Church leaders that the Church will face the Antichrist.) This historic second advent orthodoxy is also seen in the teachings of more recent Church leaders, such as John Wesley, George Whitfield, Adam Clarke, Charles Finney, and many others.

It is the consistent admonition of Scripture that believers prepare, watch, and be ready. These commands bode of hardships, persecutions, deceptions, and tribulations. Christians will indeed encounter these things in this world. Believers should give most earnest heed to a preparation that will equip them for this type of trouble. The hope of escaping the troubles that precede Christ's return is Scripturally suspect. Even more suspect than an expectant mother hoping to escape the travail of birth. We should bank on the hope that He ***that sticketh closer than a brother***[b] will go with us through the fire and bring us out of the trouble. The trouble that lies ahead is not worthy to be compared with the glory that Christians will enjoy with Christ throughout eternity. For this reason the apostle John could say, ***even so, come Lord Jesus!***[c]

---

a George E. Ladd, <u>The Blessed Hope</u>, pg. 31.

b Proverbs 18:24.

c Revelation 22:20.

PART II
SIGNS OF HIS SOON RETURN

To this point the focus of this work has been on comparing two Christian viewpoints on the second coming of Christ. Both boldly proclaim the sure return of Christ and only differ in their specific understanding of the timing of the Rapture of the Church. Each of these examined views are truly Christian. There are many God fearing, Bible believing Christians to be found on both sides of this debate. Together, both pretribulationists and posttribulationists look forward to the coming of Christ with joyous anticipation. Though there may be debate as to the timing of His coming, or about the particular things that will occur at His coming, the event itself is the precious hope of the Christians who hold to either of these viewpoints.

In the pages which follow, however, the focus has been taken off of a debate between Christian brethren. The signs that are highlighted in the following chapters are generally agreed upon in both camps. Also, the doctrinal heresies that will be examined here are abhorrent to both.

Following, are several signs given in Scripture that will signal the soon return of Christ. Most of these are taken from Christ's instruction to His disciples in the Olivet Discourse. Many of these signs may have already begun to come to pass. Ardent prayers for spiritual discernment are in order, and all Christians should be fervently lifting such prayers.

In the pages that follow I have given explanation as to my best interpretation of the meaning of each of the following signs. It should be remembered, though, that these views are merely a Christian's best estimation as to the identification and meaning of these signs. These views are certainly subject to error. Indeed, some may completely miss the mark. Each reader should use this listing as a prayer list. It is only the Holy Spirit who can give true discernment as to the identity and meaning of the signs of the times. He will give this discernment to those children who seek it with all their heart. May God grant His Church abundant grace for seeking truth and understanding in this hour.

17:   Israel's Gathering and Salvation[a]

Ezekiel 36:16-33 - [16]Moreover the word of the LORD came unto me, saying, [17]Son of man, when the house of Israel dwelt in their own land, they defiled it by their own way and by their doings: their way was before me as the uncleanness of a removed woman. [18]Wherefore I poured my fury upon them for the blood that they had shed upon the land, and for their idols wherewith they had polluted it: [19]And I scattered them among the heathen, and they were dispersed through the countries: according to their way and according to their doings I judged them. [20]And when they entered unto the heathen, whither they went, they profaned my holy name, when they said to them, These are the people of the LORD, and are gone forth out of his land.

[21]But I had pity for mine holy name, which the house of Israel had profaned among the heathen, whither they went. [22]Therefore say unto the house of Israel, Thus saith the Lord GOD; I do not this for your sakes, O house of Israel, but for mine holy name's sake, which ye have profaned among the heathen, whither ye went. [23]And I will sanctify my great name, which was profaned among the heathen, which ye have profaned in the midst of them; and the heathen shall know that I am the LORD, saith the Lord GOD, when I shall be sanctified in you before their eyes. [24]For I will take you from among the heathen, and gather you out of all countries, and will bring you into your own land.

[25]Then will I sprinkle clean water upon you, and ye shall be clean: from all your filthiness, and from all your idols, will I cleanse you. [26]A new heart also will I give you, and a new spirit will I put within you: and I will take away the stony heart out of your flesh, and I will give you an heart of flesh. [27]And I will put my spirit within you, and cause you to walk in my statutes, and ye shall keep my judgments, and do them. [28]And ye shall dwell in the land that I gave to your fathers; and ye shall be my people, and I

---

a See *Appendix A* for a listing of Scriptures which prophesy of these events.

will be your God. ²⁹I will also save you from all your uncleannesses: and I will call for the corn, and will increase it, and lay no famine upon you. ³⁰And I will multiply the fruit of the tree, and the increase of the field, that ye shall receive no more reproach of famine among the heathen. ³¹Then shall ye remember your own evil ways, and your doings that were not good, and shall loathe yourselves in your own sight for your iniquities and for your abominations. ³²Not for your sakes do I this, saith the Lord GOD, be it known unto you: be ashamed and confounded for your own ways, O house of Israel. ³³Thus saith the Lord GOD; In the day that I shall have cleansed you from all your iniquities I will also cause you to dwell in the cities, and the wastes shall be builded.

This lengthy reference is included to demonstrate the profound prophecies found in Scripture about Israel's apostasy, restoration, and redemption. These prophecies identify clear Scriptural signs which, when fulfilled, are distinct indicators of the soon return of Christ. There are several Scriptural prophecies that tell of the apostasy and dispersion of Israel and then her gathering and redemption.[a] Here, in this Ezekiel 36 text, a clear prophetic history of Israel in the last 2,500 years is revealed. It is here revealed that Israel's dispersion from the promised land was due to her iniquity and unbelief. Further, that while dwelling in foreign lands, Israel would become a byword and a reproach among all peoples due to her lowliness and pollutions. This reproach will negatively reflect upon the name of God, and thus God will gather the Israelites back to the promised land and there redeem them for His holy Name's sake.

In just their scope and detail, these prophecies are nothing less than breathtaking. When coupled with the historical perspective that the 21st century AD provides, these prophecies are simply spine tingling. From

---

a For further study please see Deuteronomy 30:1-5, Micah 4:1-10, Zephaniah 3:14-20, Zechariah 13:1-14:4, & Romans 11:25-32. These texts are included in *Appendix A*.

today's vantage point both the dispersion and re-gathering of Israel are clearly seen.

Throughout Church history many have believed that this prophecy was fulfilled when the remnant of Israel returned to the promised land in the time of Ezra and Nehemiah. There are key components, however, about this prophecy that make it clear that it has not yet been fulfilled. The New Testament refers to several Old Testament texts like this Ezekiel text, declaring that this restoration of Israel is still future.

The Apostle Paul asked the question, ***Hath God cast away his people?***[a] He then emphatically answered his own question with a firm, ***God forbid.***[b] Continuing, the Apostle Paul declared that not only has the Lord reserved a remnant of believing Israelites (such as himself), but affirms that, ***all Israel shall be saved: as it is written, There shall come out of Sion the Deliverer, and shall turn away ungodliness from Jacob: For this is my covenant unto them, when I shall take away their sins.***[c] The Apostle referred here to Isaiah 59:20-21 (***And the Redeemer shall come to Zion, and unto them that turn from transgression in Jacob, saith the LORD. As for me, this is my covenant with them, saith the LORD; My spirit that is upon thee, and my words which I have put in thy mouth, shall not depart out of thy mouth, nor out of the mouth of thy seed, nor out of the mouth of thy seed's seed, saith the LORD, from henceforth and for ever.***) and Isaiah 27:9 (***By this therefore shall the iniquity of Jacob be purged...***). So it is quite clear from Paul's declaration that these prophecies were still future at the time of his writing. And since it is still true that Israel has not yet returned unto her Messiah, these prophecies must still be understood as future.

The restoration of the Jews back to the promised land under their own sovereign government is perhaps the single greatest sign to date of Christ's soon return. It is certainly the most significant prophetic event of the last century. The re-establishment of a State of Israel in the

---

a Romans 11:1.

b Ibid.

c Romans 11:26-27.

Biblical Promised Land (Canaan or Palestine) fulfils numerous prophetic texts which foretell of this end-times event. Yet, as we see from Paul's instruction, these prophecies are only beginning to be fulfilled. The key component, Israel's salvation, is yet future.

This much, however, can be affirmed categorically: On May 28, 1948, the United Nations general assembly voted to partition Palestine creating a new and sovereign state of Israel. Suddenly, and to the astonishment of historians and political analysts, Israel was once again a geographic nation in the Biblical Promised Land and not just a dispersed people group. This U.N. decree was violently resisted by the surrounding Arab states. The Jews dwelling in Palestine,[a] immediately upon receiving the declaration of a Jewish homeland, were plunged into a desperate and bloody war for survival as surrounding Islamic countries attacked simultaneously. The Israelites miraculously came through their "War of Independence" and throughout the decades following, Israel has endured devastating wars, diabolical terror attacks, and intense geopolitical scorn and isolation. Yet, this tiny nation has emerged as a formidable military and political power. Surrounded by hostile Islamic

---

a Incidentally, the term Palestinian was, for more than a century, used primarily to refer to Jews who were living in the promised land. It has only been since the 1950's that a Muslim population has been given sole right to that name. When the Jews began significant emigration to the Promised Land in the mid 1800's it was almost wholly uninhabited, and they were the Palestinians. Those Jewish Palestinians made the land inhabitable by cultivating the soil, planting trees, and growing crops. They did this under the failed belief that England would honor numerous promises of granting them a homeland there. England, however, continued to renege on these promises because of resistance and pressure from allied Arab states.

After the 1948 U.N. decree, and after they failed to destroy the Jews by a surprise attack, the surrounding Muslim states began sending all their outcast populations to that region, promising these poor pawns that if they would drive the Jews out, they could dwell in Palestine. By deceit and selective amnesia many world states have forgotten this recent history of Palestine.

We are also led to believe that the "aggressive occupation" by the Israelis since 1967 of disputed territories such as the West Bank, Gaza Strip, and the Golan Heights is the reason for the turmoil in the Middle East. But this supposed cause of the unrest overlooks an obvious fact. In 1967 when the surrounding Arab states massed for an annihilation attack on Israel, intending to drive the Jews into the sea, Israel was not occupying any part of the currently "disputed" territories.

dictatorships, Israel stands as a free and democratic republic, and a regional superpower. These accomplishments are more than amazing, they are miraculous.

Throughout Church history many Christian scholars treated the numerous Scriptural prophecies of the "re-birth" of Israel as figurative or allegorical references to the Church. The reasons for not accepting a literal interpretation varied, but usually centered around three opinions; either a firmly fixed anti-Semitism, or a pragmatic evaluation concluding that a literal interpretation was impossible, or a belief that the Christian Church is the only possible entity that could fulfil these prophecies. These beliefs notwithstanding, the prophecies have begun to come to pass literally.

Fortunately, not all Christian scholars overlooked a literal fulfilment of these prophecies. Throughout Church history (beginning with Christ's first apostles) faithful Bible scholars have proclaimed that Israel would someday be re-gathered to the land of Canaan and would there be redeemed. This is beginning to happen and it is blessed to behold! In this literal fulfilment, Christians must see that the Lord is broadcasting a clear sign of His soon return.

Do not neglect to realize, however, that this sign of the restoration of Israel has only partially been fulfilled. As stated above, the primary component of the restoration, the redemption of Israel, has yet to come to pass. Christians should joyously look for the fruits of this sign with this anticipation: *if the casting away of* [the Jews] *be the reconciling of the world, what shall the receiving of them be, but life from the dead?*[a]

It is significant to note that Ezekiel's prophecy is very clear as to the time sequence of the events of this sign. He states that first there will be a gathering back of Jews to the Promised Land, and then the redemption of Israel will take place: *For I will take you from among the heathen, and gather you out of all countries, and will bring you into your own land. Then will I sprinkle clean water upon you, and*

---

ye shall be clean: from all your filthiness, and from all your idols, will I cleanse you.[a]

The day of this prophesied cleansing of Israel will be a glorious day for mankind. In that day there will be a great revival, not only in Israel, but also throughout all the peoples of the earth. Scripture indicates that this greatest of awakenings will be led by redeemed Israelites. The reference of the sealing of the 144,000 Israelite *servants of our God,*[b] recorded in Revelation, clearly indicates that these redeemed individuals are physical descendants of the original twelve sons of Israel (Jacob.) The Apostle John goes through great lengths to detail the number sealed from each tribe.

Although the particular area of service of these sealed servants of God is not expressly defined, it appears that they will be Jewish evangelists who proclaim the gospel in the last days.[c] Through their ministry an innumerable host of people from the very ends of the earth will be saved.[d] This is a hopeful promise that the Christian Church should confidently expect and eagerly await. After declaring the reality of the rejection of their Messiah, the Bible declares that a glorious day will come upon the earth when the physical children of Israel finally turn to Christ in salvation.[e] This will be the greatest revival in human history and it is still future.

While in captivity in Babylon, Daniel examined the prophecy of Jeremiah concerning the Babylonian captivity and realized that its duration was to be seventy years. When he understood this, he went into his prayer closet and prayed fervently for Israel's deliverance.[f] Believers should take the prophet Daniel's lead, and eagerly pray for God to bring about this promise of the last-days redemption of Israel.

---

a Ezekiel 36:24-25.

b Revelation 7:3 (full text - verses 1-8.)

c See Revelation 14:1-6.

d See Revelation 7:9.

e See Romans 11:15.

f See Daniel 9:2*ff.*

18:   Technology and Travel Rapidly Increase

Daniel 12:4 - But thou, O Daniel, shut up the words, and seal the book, even to the time of the end: many shall run to and fro, and knowledge shall be increased.

It is simply astonishing to witness the increases in technology and travel in these days. The twentieth century saw numerous quantum-leap type advancements in knowledge and transportation. Consider that the speed of a horse was the top speed of human travel for the last four-thousand years. Then, in a span of little more than a hundred years, the top speed of travel has increased to several hundred miles per hour (several thousand m.p.h. in supersonic and space travel.) The first two generations of the twentieth century saw people move from the horse and buggy age to the jet age. These rapid technological advancements are wholly unprecedented in recorded human history. From the view of world history, these days are simply amazing days.

Dr. Jack Van Impe, in his book entitled, Israel's Final Holocaust, makes the following observation:

> *"For decades, certain Orthodox rabbis have maintained that Messiah would come when three signs were in evidence at the same time.*
>
> *First, there must be speeding chariots in the streets of Jerusalem, fulfilling Nahum 2:4:* **The chariots shall rage in the streets, they shall justle one against another in the broad ways: they shall seem like torches, they shall run like the lightnings.**
>
> *This interesting verse once prompted Sir Isaac Newton to predict that men would someday travel as fast as forty miles per hour.*[a]

---

[a] This statement was based upon Newton's scientific studies to determine how fast an object would need to travel to appear as a flash of lightening as it passed a given point. Through research, he determined that the object would need to be traveling at least 40 miles per hour to achieve the flash-by effect.

Voltaire, an enemy of Christianity in that era, scorned Newton's statement, saying, 'See what a fool Christianity makes of an otherwise brilliant man, such as Sir Isaac Newton! Doesn't he know that if a man traveled forty miles an hour, he would suffocate and his heart would stop?'

But Newton was conservatively correct. And today, in Jerusalem, as in other major cities, speeding chariots (automobiles) **jostle one against another in the broad ways.** *At night they* **seem like torches** *and they run like lightening.*

The second sign, the rabbis said, would be the protection of Jerusalem by men flying as birds. **As birds flying, so will the LORD of hosts defend Jerusalem; defending also he will deliver it; and passing over he will preserve it.** *(Isa. 31:5)...*

The third requirement of the rabbis was the blossoming of the desert. **The wilderness and the solitary place shall be glad for them; and the desert shall rejoice, and blossom as the rose.** *(Isa. 35:1)."*[a]

All three of these signs are presently in place in Israel. Israel is a technologically advanced nation, and she surpasses even the U.S. and Western Europe in the implementation of new technologies. (I was in Israel in 1996 and witnessed a wide-spread use of cell phones which was not paralleled in the U.S. for at least three more years.) Soldiers in the Israeli army are equipped with the most advanced armor and computer integration. Many military experts rate the Israeli army as the most advanced in the world. Yet this use of technology and ease of travel is not limited to certain countries or regions of the world. It has fully covered the earth.

This speed and ease of travel has literally changed the human experience. From the time of Noah until just a few years ago the average man traveled little, usually living in the same area all his life. This is no longer the case. Since World War II, regional and international travel has accelerated exponentially. With this ease and speed of travel comes rapid world changes.

---

a Dr. Jack Van Impe, Israel's Final Holocaust, pgs. 21-22.

Since the splitting of the atom these rapid changes have increased greatly in frequency. The phenomenon of computer technology is perhaps even more astounding. The increase in the store of human knowledge since the advent of computers is many times greater than the sum of all human knowledge stores compiled from all the centuries since the Noahic Flood. Add to this the Internet, cell phone technology, remote computing technology, and the possibilities for knowledge increase and information exchange literally border on the infinite. It is virtually impossible to keep up with these advancements in technology. Computers seem to be out-of-date from the moment of purchase. It requires almost a daily vigilance just to keep abreast of these changes.

Yet this technical progress and global travel has not escaped the pages of Holy Writ. God's Word teaches that this sudden increase of knowledge and travel is a sign of the ***time of the end.***[a] This rapid increase of knowledge and travel indicates that man is in the final days of this world system. As a race, we are on the verge of seeing the Messianic Kingdom ushered in. Hallelujah!

There is one other intriguing component of this sign. The Daniel 12:4 text declares that the prophecies of the end are sealed and will not be unsealed until the time of the end. Isn't it interesting that modern technology has given illumination to certain Biblical prophecies? For instance, in Revelation 11 the ministry of the two faithful witnesses is recorded.[b] After they complete their testimony they will be martyred. The Bible declares that their martyred bodies will lie in the streets of Jerusalem for 3½ days. While lying there, all the people of the earth will see them and will rejoice over them.[c] How could we understand this prophecy without the knowledge of modern technology. Satellite television has made this possible, but it would not be possible without this medium. Evidently modern technology will provide at least one aspect of this unsealing of Biblical prophecies.

---

a Daniel 12:4.

b See Revelation 11:3-12

c See Revelation 11:8-10

19: Wars and International Crises

Mark 13:8 - For nation shall rise against nation, and kingdom against kingdom...

Jesus said that in the time of the end there shall be ***upon the earth distress of nations.***[a] Yet, it is hard to determine by this sign alone a specific time reference to the end times. We might say that this sign and the next, "Natural Calamities," are secondary or corresponding signs. The time of the end will include global wars and unrest and will include great natural disasters. However, these events, on their own, may not clearly signal the end times. It seems that in each generation some Christians have had to endure the horrors of war or disaster. This has led many to wrongly conclude in their day that, "Surely, these are the very last days." The days just prior to Christ's return will include the devastations of war and grave natural calamities, but will also include other, more specific, signs. Remember, Jesus has identified this time of proliferating war and distress as ***the beginning of sorrows.***[b]

However, it does appear that a distinct component of the time of the end will be unprecedented international distress and warfare. Connected to the next several signs, it may be that the abounding of iniquity and the diminishing of love will make the time of the end a particularly hostile time. The Lord revealed that the condition of man on earth at the time of the end will be similar to his condition at the time of Noah.[c] Scripture describes the evil time in which Noah lived in this way: ***The earth also was corrupt before God, and the earth was _filled with violence_. And God looked upon the earth, and, behold, it was corrupt; for all flesh had corrupted his way upon the earth. And God said unto Noah, The end of all flesh is come before me; for the earth is _filled with violence_ through them; and, behold, I will destroy them***

---

a Luke 21:25.

b Matthew 24:8.

c See Matthew 24:37 & Luke 17:26.

with the earth.[a] Two times in these three verses the Lord referenced the violence on earth. He specifically said that He was about to destroy the earth because of this violence.

The mixture of the iniquity that resides in the fallen human heart with the efficiencies of human destruction that modern weaponry affords and the ease of access to these *"weapons of mass destruction,"* have brewed an elixir of woe. It seems that men of the last days will either be unwilling or unable to avoid drinking this evil potion.

An objective and cursory examination of human history over the last one hundred and fifty years demonstrates that man's mournful inclination to develop new ways to kill his fellow man has risen to unheard of and previously inconceivable dimensions. The twentieth century was a particularly bloody century. The wars and government sponsored killings of that century have no equal. It appears that the **beginning of sorrows**[b] has already begun.

Seeming to start with the American Civil War, man has also witnessed a *"science of killing machines"* that has resulted in weapons that are literally able to eliminate human life on earth. Developed at the end of the nineteenth century, the machine gun has the dubious distinction of being a most effective killing machine. Many analysts have noted that this one weapon type may be responsible for more human deaths than any other.

Of course, the specter of nuclear warfare makes all other weapons and war implements pale by comparison. Given the violence that is in man, it is hard to imagine a way of avoiding doomsday type conflicts in the immediate future. Again quoting Dr. Van Impe, *"In 1860, a French scientist named Pierre Berchelt predicted: 'Within a hundred years of physical and chemical science, man will know what the atom is. It is my belief that when science reaches this stage, God will say to humanity: 'Gentlemen, it is closing time'"*[c]

---

a Genesis 6:11-13.

b Mark 13:8.

c Dr. Jack Van Impe, Israel's Final Holocaust, pg. 13.

Prudence, it seems, directs us to believe that this ominous progression in the magnitude and frequency of warfare is a distinct indicator that man is indeed in the last days. It is true that man has been a warring creature since the Fall, yet the proficiency with which human destruction is planned and executed in these days is an evident token that the ***day of the Lord***[a] is fast approaching.

One final observation on this sign: In the twentieth century the wars were generally political in nature. Yet, at the dawn of the twenty-first century, there appears to be a new and ominous trend emerging, that of religious warfare. There seems to be no passions of the heart of man that equal the potential ferocity of religious passions. The world appears to be at the verge of exploding in religious strife, and that specter will surely have the potential to make even politically motivated warfare tame by comparison.

---

a 1 Thessalonians 5:2.

20: Increase of Natural Calamities

Mark 13:8 - ...[T]here shall be earthquakes in divers places, and there shall be famines and troubles: these are the beginnings of sorrows.

*Luke 21:25-27 - *²⁵*And there shall be signs in the sun, and in the moon, and in the stars; and upon the earth distress of nations, with perplexity; the sea and the waves roaring;* ²⁶*Men's hearts failing them for fear, and for looking after those things which are coming on the earth: for the powers of heaven shall be shaken. *²⁷*And then shall they see the Son of man coming in a cloud with power and great glory.*

This, indeed, is an intriguing sign of the end times. However, an examination of world history indicates that catastrophic natural disasters wax and wane in frequency. It seems that there are certain time periods on earth (perhaps hundreds of years in length) of relative calm, then there are periods of many catastrophes. The time of the end will be a time of unprecedented natural disasters, but the ability to use this as a specific indicator is limited. Because of the ebb and flow of these global cycles, it may be hard for the believers living in the last days to know the certainty of this sign. Also remember that this sign, as with the previous, is described as *the beginning of sorrows.*[a]

Again it appears that the signs of war and disaster will be indistinct on their own. Only when these events are coupled with the other signs of the end times will they have specific pertinence. However, there is clear indication that there will be specific cosmic indicators announcing the very time of the end. The Luke reference, included above, describes certain cosmic events to be immediate precursors of Christ's actual coming. What these signs will be is not clear, but the alert believer will apparently be able to identify them in that day.

---

a Matthew 24:8.

One hint to the identification of these celestial signs may be found in the recording of the third trumpet judgment found in Revelation 8:10-11. This judgment involved an impact on earth by an asteroid or comet called **Wormwood**.[a] The potential of earth receiving a devastating strike from a celestial body is being increasingly examined by the scientific community. These scientific inquiries seem to lead to only one conclusion, namely, this planet is highly vulnerable to the ravages of a large meteor strike. It was only a few years ago that this potentiality was wholly unknown, but it has recently risen in the estimation of many astronomical scientists as one of the gravest dangers facing the planet.

This earth seems also to be showing signs of stress. The size of the earth's deserts is growing, the level of the earth's oceans is rising, and the stress on the earth's surface appears to be increasing. Though the potential causes of these conditions are the subject of much debate, the results of these phenomena seem to be widely agreed upon. According to the scientific community, included among these consequences are violent weather patterns and the increase in the frequency and force of earthquakes and volcanos.

In summary, throughout Church history believers and scoffers alike have wondered about the significance of wars and natural disasters in relation to end times prophecies. One thing, however, seems certain, the time of the end will include a time of many natural disasters. The Bible reveals that these events will be cataclysmic and will be spread out over all the earth, indeed, even in unusual (**divers**) places.

---

a See Revelation 8:11.

21: Christians Hated of All Nations

Matthew 24:9-10 - ⁹Then shall they deliver you up to be afflicted, and shall kill you: and ye shall be hated of all nations for my name's sake. ¹⁰And then shall many be offended, and shall betray one another, and shall hate one another.

The rise in the persecution of Christians in these days is very grievous to behold. Christian historians have suggested that more believers were martyred for their faith in the twentieth century than in all the previous nineteen centuries combined. There seems to be no relenting of this persecution as the twenty-first century begins. The attempted *"genocides"* in parts of Africa and Asia in recent years should be more properly termed *"faith-ocides;"* for these attacks have often been motivated by a religious hatred of the Christian faith of the targeted populations.

Though the secular media rarely reports this fact, most of the horrendous blood-baths that have been witnessed in recent years have been perpetrated in countries were Muslim populations have come to power. Once gaining the military wherewithal, the leaders then turn this power onto their own populations and seek to purge the *"Christian infidel"* from their midst. These zealots conduct their hellish business with a sickening efficiency, and perpetrate it under the deluded conviction that they are doing God's bidding. Jesus warned His disciples of this with these words, ***the time cometh, that whosoever killeth you will think that he doeth God service.***[a] The graphic fulfillment of Christ's prophetic warning is reported regularly on the evening news, though not always identified as such.

This same goal of eradicating the Christian faith was behind much of the persecution and martyrdom that occurred in communist countries in the last half of the twentieth century. China is a particularly onerous example. Christian missionaries were expelled from China in the late

---

a John 16:2.

1940's. That expulsion signaled the beginning of a horrendous period of persecution. Estimates vary widely, but the two decades that followed may have marked the single greatest period in world history to date, for Christian martyrdom. The estimates of the victims of these atrocities range into the tens of millions. In the late 1950's it is believed that over thirty-thousand Christians were crucified on makeshift crosses in a region in southern China.

Yet, this horrific and continuing persecution of Chinese Christians also stands as a glorious example of how Christ will build His Church even in the midst of great persecution. (*I will build my church; and the gates of hell shall not prevail against it.*[a]) It is estimated that the total number of Christians in China in 1948 was around one million. In five-plus decades of repression, persecution, and martyrdom, that number has burgeoned one-hundredfold, to an estimated one-hundred million Christians!

Scripture reveals that this phenomenon will also occur during the Tribulation. This time of trouble that is coming will be the most severe time of persecution and martyrdom of saints in world history. (*For then shall be great tribulation, such as was not since the beginning of the world to this time, no, nor ever shall be. And except those days should be shortened, there should no flesh be saved: but for the elect's sake those days shall be shortened.*[b]) Yet, it may also be the single greatest period of salvation in human history, for a host which cannot be numbered by man will be saved during that time. (*After this I beheld, and, lo, a great multitude, which no man could number, of all nations, and kindreds, and people, and tongues, stood before the throne, and before the Lamb, clothed with white robes, and palms in their hands; And cried with a loud voice, saying, Salvation to our God which sitteth upon the throne, and unto the Lamb. ...And one of the elders answered, saying unto me, What are these which are arrayed in white robes? and whence came they? And I said unto him, Sir, thou*

---

a Matthew 16:18.

b Matthew 24:21-22.

***knowest. And he said to me, These are they which came out of great tribulation, and have washed their robes, and made them white in the blood of the Lamb.**[a]*)

Please notice another thing about this sign. Jesus precisely said that His followers would be hated ***of all nations.**[b]* It seems significant that Jesus specifically mentioned that the ***nations*** would hate those who are called Christian (***for my name's sake.**[c]*) A study of recent world history reveals an interesting trend. Nations, not just individuals, are becoming more and more anti-Christian. The official position of Muslim, Buddhist, and Hindu countries is increasingly becoming expressly hostile to Christianity.

However, it does not stop there. It may surprise many readers to discover that most "Christian" nations have recently moved to decidedly anti-Christian positions. This is often accomplished under the guise of being "secular," or "pluralistic." Yet, the particular religion that is singled out to be purged from the official national psyche is invariably the Christian religion. There was a time when many of these countries were officially Christian. Then they moved to being officially secular. Now it appears that they are becoming officially anti-Christian. The recent history of western European countries, France in particular, provides many egregious examples of this transition. Though this trend is ignored or denied by many in positions of authority, nevertheless, a fair assessment of the facts leads to no other conclusion.

Though not nearly as far advanced as in Europe, this trend is also evident in the United States. Under the banner of "Separation of Church and State,"[d] there is a systematic effort underway, by such groups as the People for the American Way and the American Civil Liberties Union (ACLU) to simply erase America's Christian

---

a Revelation 7:9-10, 13-14.

b Matthew 24:9.

c Ibid.

d This phrase is not found in the U.S. Constitution, the Bill of Rights, or in any other official founding document of the United States.

foundation and heritage from the public consciousness. Fearing lawsuits, many in such fields as business and education have simply self-censored Christ and Christianity out of their lexicons. Indeed, some have noted that the only bigotry still politically acceptable in America is anti-Christian bigotry.

Take, for example, the celebration of Christmas in many public schools. Just a few years ago, relatively speaking, major Christmas pageants were the norm in the public schools of America. Now they are the exception. At the same time the celebration of Halloween has mushroomed. Yet, the religious nature of both of these holidays is unmistakable. Thus, this is the apparent message, it is politically correct in public schools to celebrate and promote a holiday sacred in the Wiccan Religion, but unacceptable to promote a religious holiday precious to the vast majority of Americans. Some will counter by asserting that Halloween is a Christian holiday also. But I ask, what particulars of that holiday promote Christianity in any way? We can find abundant examples of the celebration of witchcraft and the promotion of paganism in it, but I am at a loss to find anything Christian about it.

22: False Christs and False Prophets Abound

Matthew 24:4-5 - ⁴And Jesus answered and said unto them, Take heed
that no man deceive you. ⁵For many shall come in my name,
saying, I am Christ; and shall deceive many.

Matthew 24:11 - And many false prophets shall rise, and shall deceive
many.

Matthew 24:24 - For there shall arise false Christs, and false
prophets, and shall show great signs and wonders; insomuch that,
if it were possible, they shall deceive the very elect.

In answering the three-fold question of the disciples which
precipitated the Olivet Discourse, the first warning from the Lord was
of deception. The Bible records, *as* [Jesus] *sat upon the mount of*
Olives, the disciples came unto him privately, saying, Tell us, when
shall these things be? and what shall be the sign of thy coming, and
of the end of the world?[a] Jesus then delivered a precise caution to the
disciples that they should prepare for deception. In the discourse, Christ
stated this warning of preparing for deception three times. This sign of
His coming is the only one that Jesus repeated. Apparently the Lord
wanted His followers to be aware that great deception would precede
His coming.

It is sure that false Christs and false prophets have always assailed
the Church. Believers in the time of the Apostles dealt with them, and
every generation of Christians since then has had to endure them.
However, the distinct admonition of Christ is that in the last days these
deceivers will be particularly prevalent and malevolent.

The fact of this coming deception identifies perhaps the most
sobering and compelling reason for believers to be spiritually alert.
Discernment is not a function of the mind, it is a function of the spirit.

---

a Matthew 24:3.

Discernment is the first thing that is lost when a Christian delves into disobedience or sloth. The Scripture commands believers to *Be sober, be vigilant; because your adversary the devil, as a roaring lion, walketh about, seeking whom he may devour: Whom resist stedfast in the faith...*[a] Christians are responsible to be those *who by reason of use have their senses exercised to discern both good and evil.*[b]

Remember that a deceiver does not walk around with an identifying neon sign on his forehead. By definition, deceivers knowingly mislead. The designation of, *false prophets,* means that these charlatans will be in the pulpits of the Church. Christians are not likely to be deceived by people who openly espouse heresies or other religions. Deception will come from the wolves in sheep's clothing. (*Beware of false prophets, which come to you in sheep's clothing, but inwardly they are ravening wolves.*[c])

For these reasons, believers must have a Berean frame of mind. The Bible testifies of the spiritual diligence of the Jews of Berea in this way: *These were more noble than those in Thessalonica, in that they received the word with all readiness of mind, and searched the scriptures daily, whether those things were so.*[d] Also, Jesus commended the Church at Ephesus because they had *tried them which say they are apostles, and are not, and hast found them liars.*[e] Many Christians who have neglected this duty need now to own up to this obligation! Unimaginable heresies flourish today in the pulpits of the Church. Some of the blame for this must rest at the feet of those who have assumed it is someone else's responsibility to examine the Scriptural soundness of the things that they are being taught. Jesus put the responsibility squarely on the shoulders of His followers. He said, *Take heed that no man deceive you.*[f]

---

a 1 Peter 5:8-9.

b Hebrews 5:14.

c Matthew 7:15.

d Acts 17:11.

e Revelation 2:2.

f Matthew 24:4.

God has called all Christians to study His Word, which is a divine road map for navigating through the pitfalls of deception. He promises the Spirit's wisdom to those who ask for it in simple faith. Yet, many Christians seem to think they have no need of utilizing these provisions. It is time for each child of God to pray for grace that the Lord help him to *Study to show* [himself] *approved unto God, a workman that needeth not to be ashamed, rightly dividing the word of truth.*[a]

---

[a] 2 Timothy 2:15.

23:   Iniquity Abounds and Love Diminishes

Matthew 24:12 - And because iniquity shall abound, the love of many shall wax cold.

This sign is among the most troubling of all that Jesus gave to His disciples, and a precise understanding of the nature of iniquity is necessary to correctly interpret it. Iniquity is frequently used in the context of gross sin and is, therefore, often considered simply a synonym for sin in excess. Its precise meaning, however, is much more basic to man's fallen nature.

Iniquity is, in reality, the condition of heart of man that causes sin. Perhaps the best single-sentence definition of iniquity in all of Scripture is found in Isaiah 51:6. The verse states, *All we like sheep have gone astray; we have turned every one to his own way; and the LORD hath laid on him the iniquity of us all.*

Iniquity, then, is man going his own way; man doing what he wants; man *"looking out for number one."* That basic intent of the fallen human heart will indeed lead to the vilest sin. Yet, iniquity is in the heart long before any great perversions are committed, because iniquity is the basic pride, selfishness, and self-conceit that is the default heart-condition of fallen man.

A Scriptural search for the essence of sin will invariably arrive at pride or self-conceit. Man's pride is the culprit that led Jesus Christ to the cross. In reality, pride and self-conceit may be accurately said to be the source of all sin.

"Doing it my way," is the normal course for mankind. Since the fall, and as a race, man has this inclination. It was inherited from father Adam and remains in full force in this generation.

David understood this perilous condition of his heart when he prayed his prayer of repentance recorded in Psalm 51. He stated, *Behold, I was shapen in iniquity, and in sin did my mother conceive me.*[a] David was not accusing his mother of some secret sin or

---

a Psalm 51:5.

perversion, nor was he trying to blame his sin on his parents. Rather, he was proclaiming a basic understanding about his fallen nature. He knew this condition was damnable. He was acutely aware of his problem and knew he desperately needed to be forgiven and cleansed. In short, he needed a remedy for his iniquitous condition.

Iniquity is often at its worst without any open or vile sin being present. Jesus said that in judgment there will be many people that will come to Him proclaiming that they had done many good works for Him. Nevertheless, the Lord will say that they were workers of iniquity: (*Many will say to me in that day, Lord, Lord, have we not prophesied in thy name? and in thy name have cast out devils? and in thy name done many wonderful works? And then will I profess unto them, I never knew you: depart from me, ye that work iniquity.*[a])

How does a person do things like prophesy, or cast out devils, or perform many wonderful works, and do them as works of iniquity? The answer is, when these works are done for self-glory or by self-will. With that motive they are works of iniquity.

Great cathedrals can be erected and the hungry can be fed as works of iniquity.[b] Even the preaching of the gospel can be a work of iniquity.[c] If these things are done for motives of self-will or of self-glory then they are iniquitous works.

Now couple this understanding with the cause-effect sequence that Jesus gives here as a sign of the end (*because iniquity shall abound, the love of many shall wax cold.*[d]) The best way to dampen the love or goodwill of others is to do something with a self-serving motive. A hidden agenda of self advancement will simply cause love (at least human love) to evaporate.

Indeed, the Bible reveals that perilous times will come in the last days because of self-love. (*This know also, that in the last days*

---

a Matthew 7:22-23.

b See 1 Corinthians 13:1-3 for a list of several "good" things that can be done with iniquitous or loveless motives.

c See Philippians 1:15-16.

d Matthew 24:12.

perilous times shall come. **For men shall be lovers of their own selves**, *covetous, boasters, proud, blasphemers, disobedient to parents, unthankful, unholy, Without natural affection, trucebreakers, false accusers, incontinent, fierce, despisers of those that are good, Traitors, heady, highminded, lovers of pleasures more than lovers of God; Having a form of godliness, but denying the power thereof: from such turn away.*[a])

It is interesting that one of the most common "sacred mantras" in modern psychology, even "Christian psychology," is the "need to promote self-love or self-esteem." At the very time in history when the Scriptures warn that *men shall be lovers of their own selves,*[b] these modern white robed priests of humanism say that man has a shortage of self-love. Even from Christian pulpits or counseling centers the answer for the emptiness, depression, and aimlessness that man, separated from God by sin, faces is a recipe of self-love, or self-acceptance, or self-esteem, or self-forgiveness. The Christian gospel of turning in repentance from self to God is being drowned out by these selfisms.

A common teaching proclaimed from inside the Church is that men need to learn to love themselves first before they can love others or God. The timeless orthodoxy that declares man in his fallen state to be consumed with pride and self-will has suddenly fallen out of favor even in many Christian Churches.

This promotion of self-love is wholly at odds with the Christian gospel. God has established an absolute standard for how one person is to love another, *Thou shalt love thy neighbour as thyself.*[c] This is a comparative standard, and in order for it to be effective there must be no question about man's love of self. Simply put, if a person cannot look to how he loves himself as an instructor for how he is to love his neighbor, than he has no direction as to how he should love his neighbor. If self-love is capricious, as many teach, than Jesus erected

---

a 2 Timothy 3:1-5.

b 2 Timothy 3:2.

c See Leviticus 19:18, Matthew 19:19, 22:39, Mark 12:31, Romans 13:9, Galatians 5:14, & James 2:8.

a very fallible standard for how we are to love one another. But of course, Jesus did no such thing. There is no question about man's love of self. All men love themselves. It is impossible not to love yourself.

Yet many who claim to profess established truth, teach that men must learn to love themselves. This is simply not true; ***For no man ever yet hated his own flesh; but nourisheth and cherisheth it.***[a] Humans do not have a problem of lack of self love. Their problem is all the other way.

In his book, The Seduction of Christianity, Dave Hunt makes the following observation about the fallen condition of man and the modern deceptive teachings that are promoting self love:

> *"For 1900 years the church has taught that we are innately self-centered beings who do not need to learn to love ourselves. What we are urged to do is to love God and others... Yet through the influence of... psychologists, the church has now accepted the idea that when Jesus said, "Love your neighbor as yourself," He was teaching that we must 'learn to love ourselves first of all' before we can love God or our neighbor...*
>
> *"Biblical exhortations not to think too highly of self, when interpreted in light of modern psychology, are understood actually to be admonitions against esteeming ourselves too lowly. And those who fail to accept this new gospel 'just don't know their psychology,' even though they may be very mature in their understanding of Scripture. To encourage selfism in creatures whose besetting sins are all centered in self is like pouring gasoline on a fire that is already raging out of control."*[b]

After fittingly commenting that if indeed such an *"epidemic of inferiority"*[c] exists today this would be the first generation in human history to suffer such a malady, he then exposed the folly of believing

---

a Ephesians 5:29.

b Dave Hunt & T. A. McMahon, The Seduction of Christianity, pg. 201.

c Ibid, p. 198.

that this supposed human condition actually exists. He powerfully drove this point home with the following comments:

"The person who says, 'I'm so ugly, I hate myself!' doesn't hate himself at all, or he would be glad that he was ugly. It is because he loves himself that he is upset with his appearance and the way people respond to him. The person who grovels in depression and says he hates himself for having wasted his life would actually be glad that he had wasted his life if he really hated himself. In fact, he is unhappy about having wasted his life because he loves himself... So it is with the person who takes his own life. Most of these tragic people consider suicide to be an escape; but who helps someone he hates to escape?"[a]

The Lord gave the Church an ominous warning in this sign of His coming. The sharp rise of iniquity (unchecked self-love and self-gratification) will correspond with the fading of love for others. It is in this day that Christ's love, ministered through Christ's ambassadors, is so vitally needed. May God help His Church to be truly perfected in the love of God, for that attribute of the Almighty is desperately wanting in this world.

Please do not overlook the possible connection between this sign and the releasing of the ***mystery of iniquity***[b] which is directly related to the emergence of the Antichrist. It has always been a source of wonder to realize that the Antichrist will be able to unify the myriad of world religions into one global religion. How will this be accomplished? There is so much antagonism within the various religions of the world that it is hard to imagine civility even at that level. For example, resolving the hostility that exists between the Sunni and Shia sects of Islam or certain Protestant and Catholic groups in Christianity is hard to envision. It is much more unimaginable to see the animosity and hostility that endures between religions resolved. Of a surety this will be among the greatest "wonders" that the Antichrist will perform.

---

a Dave Hunt & T. A. McMahon, The Seduction of Christianity, pgs. 199-200.
b See 2 Thessalonians 2:7.

Yet, a clue to this conundrum may be found in this warning about how iniquity will abound in the last days. Remembering the definition of iniquity, it may be that the method which this *son of perdition* will use to unify mankind behind him is the age old method of flattery. Could it be that his most effective coercion tactic will be to simply give to men what their iniquity is craving, adulation and praise? The Antichrist may do the very thing that many cult leaders and politicians have done through the ages. Politicians and political movements are often built up by and lubricated with flattery. Even whole false religious systems have been erected upon flattery and the promise to followers of attaining godhood. The faithful are assured of achieving this divine status if they diligently follow the instructions or imitate the actions of their master (guru, shaman, leader). It is good to remember the instruction of Scripture here, *A man that flattereth his neighbour spreadeth a net for his feet.*[a]

After displaying incredible supernatural power, the *man of sin* may simply employ this age old tactic. He could promise his deluded followers, *"You can do what I do, you can become what I am, if you simply worship me."* Remember, Eve was allured by a promise to become like God when she succumbed to the serpent's beguiling lies in the Garden of Eden. Lucifer had said in his heart, *I will ascend into heaven, I will exalt my throne above the stars of God: I will sit also upon the mount of the congregation, in the sides of the north: I will ascend above the heights of the clouds; I will be like the most High.*[b] He was then summarily cast out of heaven. Having fallen to earth, he tempted Eve in the Garden with the same deception: *God doth know that in the day ye eat thereof, then your eyes shall be opened, and ye shall be as gods, knowing good and evil. And when the woman saw that the tree was good for food, and that it was pleasant to the eyes, and a tree to be desired to make one wise, she took of the fruit thereof, and did eat, and gave also unto her husband with her; and he did eat.*[c]

---

a Proverbs 29:5

b Isaiah 14:13-14.

c Genesis 3:5-6.

It is quite likely that the ***mystery of iniquity*** and the *abounding of iniquity* are directly connected. For this reason, may the children of God daily pray the very prayer of their Master, ***not my will, but thine, be done.***[a] Calvary stands in profound contrast to man's natural way. Man naturally chooses to follow his own will. Jesus chose the Father's will. Man's iniquity was laid on Christ on Golgotha's hill. In Christ there is complete deliverance, not only from the guilt of sin, but also from its power. When Isaiah's lips were cleansed the angel said ***thine iniquity is taken away, and thy sin purged.***[b] In this cleansing of Isaiah God foreshadowed the sanctifying power of Christ's redemption. This sanctifying power is available to ever child of God and is desperately needed in these last days.

Christians, you are called to live as ***lambs among wolves.***[c] In this day of perilous iniquity, the child of God is to stand as a beacon of purity, hope, and redemption. Christ has empowered you to this high calling and has commissioned you as His ambassador. ***And God is able to make all grace abound toward you; that ye, always having all sufficiency in all things, may abound to every good work:***[d]

---

a Luke 22:42.

b Isaiah 6:7.

c Luke 10:3.

d 2 Corinthians 9:8.

24: The Gospel Preached in All the World

Matthew 24:14 - And this gospel of the kingdom shall be preached in all the world for a witness unto all nations; and then shall the end come.

In the light of the previous and foregoing indicators, this sign stands as a bastion of hope and source of rejoicing! Indeed, of all the signs that Jesus left the Church in the Olivet Discourse marking His soon return, this is perhaps the most exciting. It is certainly one of the few positive indicators.

There are two amazing realities surrounding this sign. The first is the astonishing truth that in the twenty centuries since Christ's ascension the Church has not yet been able to saturate the world with the gospel. It seems unbelievable, nevertheless, it is the sobering reality that the Church of Christ must face. There have always been certain sections of the globe that have been seemingly unreachable, even untouchable.

But, Church of Christ, take hope! Now, at the beginning of the third millennium since the Lord left the Church with the great commission to go *into all the world, and preach the gospel to every creature,*[a] it appears that the Church is on the verge of truly carrying the gospel *unto the uttermost part of the earth.*[b] This fact is the second astounding component of this blessed signal of Christ's soon return.

The generation of Christians that actually witnesses the gospel's proclamation *unto the uttermost part of the earth*, is also the generation that will witness the return of Christ! This seems the unmistakable instruction of this sign. Jesus told the disciples concisely, *this gospel of the kingdom shall be preached in all the world for a witness unto all nations; and then shall the end come*. There is a connected sequence here. When the gospel is fully preached Jesus will return. Glory to His name!

---

a Mark 16:15.

b Acts 1:8.

In light of this it is exciting to realize that in recent years missiologists have identified the final unreached and under-reached people groups of earth. Strategies for reaching these peoples are in place and being worked in a surprisingly effective manner. Many different Christian denominations and organizations are working together as never before to see that this great work is completed. Many experts involved in this great global evangelistic effort predict that the whole world will be reached with the good news of Christ's redemption by the first few years of the twenty-first century. Hallelujah!

In the midst of all the woeful predicators of Christ's soon return, this sign stands as a welcome relief. Jesus said, *I will build my church; and the gates of hell shall not prevail against it.*[a] The verity and power of this proclamation is nowhere better revealed than in seeing it fulfilled at the same time in history when the *mystery of iniquity*[b] is being unleashed. As noted above, this sign will come to pass when Christians are *hated of all nations for* [Christ's] *name's sake.*[c] Though this sign seems incongruous with many of the preceding and foregoing signs, this is very consistent with the wisdom from above. Remember the Lord's words as He commissioned the seventy preachers, *Go your ways: behold, I send you forth as lambs among wolves.*[d] These lambs, armed with Christ's weapons, will accomplish what no lion or bear could do. As in every age, so in the last days, the Church will storm the very gates of hell! Jesus will continue to build His Church in the very last days, all the forces of hell notwithstanding!

Though the Lord did not reveal to His disciples the time of His return, He did specifically state that He would return in the time when the gospel truly reaches to the ends of the earth. It is a source of utmost rejoicing to see this sign coming to pass in these days!

Dear Christian, pray for your missionaries! Give to missions! Answer the missionary call! In so doing you are hurrying the blessed hope of the Church. Amen!

---

a Matthew 16:18.

b 2 Thessalonians 2:7.

c Matthew 24:9.

d Luke 10:3.

25: The Great Apostasy

1 Timothy 4:1 - Now the Spirit speaketh expressly, that in the latter times some shall depart from the faith, giving heed to seducing spirits, and doctrines of devils.

One of the distinct signs given in Scripture as an indicator of the soon return of Christ is that a great apostasy from the one true faith will occur in the Church. There are several references that foretell of this "falling away" from the faith.[a] The book of Jude is wholly dedicated to warning Christians of this hellish event. That book also reveals the essence of this great apostasy. The apostasy will be promoted by deceivers who will corrupt the understanding of the grace of God which will lead to lasciviousness or licentiousness. Jude warned, *For there are certain men crept in unawares, who were before of old ordained to this condemnation, ungodly men, <u>turning the grace of our God into lasciviousness, and denying the only Lord God, and our Lord Jesus Christ.</u>[b]* We know that this is especially a last days event because Jude noted, *Enoch also, the seventh from Adam, prophesied of these, saying, Behold, the Lord cometh with ten thousands of his saints, To execute judgment upon all, and to convince all that are ungodly among them of all their ungodly deeds which they have ungodly committed, and of all their hard speeches which ungodly sinners have spoken against him.[c]* These Scriptures make it clear that just before *the Lord cometh with ten thousands of his saints*, there will be a pervasive apostasy in the Church that will lead many to corrupt themselves while believing that Christ will wink at their defilements because of His grace. By this belief they will reject the cleansing power of Christ's redemption. Jude also warned, *Beloved, remember ye the words which were spoken before of the apostles of our Lord Jesus*

---

a See 2 Thessalonians 2:1-3, 2 Timothy 3:1*ff*, 2 Peter 2:1-22, 3:3-4, & Jude.

b Jude 1:4.

c Jude 1:14-15.

Christis; How that they told you there should be mockers in the last time, who should walk after their own ungodly lusts.[a]

The Apostle Paul also admonished the Church about this deception in his letter to the Romans. The apostle asked the question, ***What shall we say then? Shall we continue in sin, that grace may abound?***[b] He then emphatically responded, ***God forbid. How shall we, that are dead to sin, live any longer therein?***[c] The remainder of Romans chapter six is dedicated to proclaiming the glorious news of the Christian's victory over sin by the power of Christ.

I pray that all Christians would know that they need not win the victory over sin. That victory was won for them two-thousand years ago on the cross of Calvary. The great need for the Christian is to enter into the victory of Christ; the believer needs only to have the Holy Ghost do in him, what Christ has done for him on the cross. Christians are called to be witnesses[d] of Christ's redemption, we can only do that if we enter into the victory of Christ!

In his devotional, "My Utmost for His Highest," Oswald Chambers noted, *"I receive from God the gift of the Holy Spirit Who begins to interpret to me what Jesus did; and does in me subjectively all that Jesus Christ did for me objectively."*[e] He also declared, *"The Holy Spirit is the One Who makes real in you all that Jesus did for you."*[f]

The deception spoken of in Jude and Romans seems to be burgeoning in the Church today. Many speak of God's "love" and "forgiveness" but seem to overlook His holiness and cleansing power. God is not pleased to see His redeemed bride defiled by sin. He is pleased to wash her from her filthiness.[g] The Lord has given overcoming power to the redeemed. This same overcoming power is

---

a Jude 1:17-18.

b Romans 6:1.

c Romans 6:2.

d See Acts 1:8

e Oswald Chambers, My Utmost for His Highest, November 9.

f Ibid, June 9.

g See Ezekiel 36:25-26 for a declaration of the power of Christ's redemption.

expected to be at work in the life of the Christian: *He that overcometh shall inherit all things; and I will be his God, and he shall be my son. But the fearful, and unbelieving, and the abominable, and murderers, and whoremongers, and sorcerers, and idolaters, and all liars, shall have their part in the lake which burneth with fire and brimstone: which is the second death.*[a]

---

a Revelation 21:7-8.

26: A One-World Religion and Government

Revelation 13:3-4 - [3]And I saw one of his heads as it were wounded to death; and his deadly wound was healed: and all the world wondered after the beast. [4]And they worshipped the dragon which gave power unto the beast: and they worshipped the beast, saying, Who is like unto the beast? who is able to make war with him?

Revelation 13:16-17 - [16]And he causeth all, both small and great, rich and poor, free and bond, to receive a mark in their right hand, or in their foreheads: [17]And that no man might buy or sell, save he that had the mark, or the name of the beast, or the number of his name.

The Almighty proclaimed in His Word that one distinct sign of His divine power is that He knows the end from the beginning. (***Remember the former things of old: for I am God, and there is none else; I am God, and there is none like me, Declaring the end from the beginning, and from ancient times the things that are not yet done, saying, My counsel shall stand, and I will do all my pleasure:***[a]) Scripture also declares, ***Surely the Lord GOD will do nothing, but he revealeth his secret unto his servants the prophets.***[b] These divine proclamations are astoundingly apropos to this very day. Thousands of years ago God declared, through His ***servants the prophets***, that a one-world super-state would emerge on the world scene just before His return. The reality of this global super-state is not only conceivable in a practical way in this day, it is actually coming to pass. May the grace of God be brought to bare on the world's agnostics and skeptics. This one prophecy of Scripture, which is being fulfilled in this generation, should be sufficient to cause all men to fall ***on their faces: and*** [say], ***The LORD, he is the God; the LORD, he is the God.***[c]

---

a Isaiah 46:9-10.

b Amos 3:7.

c 1 Kings 18:39.

Is it not utterly amazing that in these days the very technology and human desire to sustain such a world-wide kingdom is in place? Since WWII *"globalist"* leaders from virtually every nation on earth have worked to see this global super-state advanced. Under the guise of preventing war, pollution, famine, and other troubles and abuses, a generation of the world's brightest political minds have seemingly been solely bent on this one priority. The elimination of national boundaries is promoted in school textbooks the world over as not just a possibility, but as a desirable and workable probability that the *"citizens of the world"* should see as their duty to advance! Politicians are judged by their ability or inability to work with and advance this *"world community."* This *"global consciousness"* is a very new thing by world history standards.

A primary tactical argument used to advance this one-world super-state ideal is the *"environmental protection"* argument. According to the promoters of an emerging *"religious environmentalism"* the earth is now on the verge of destruction. The fault for this impending doom is laid at the feet of the world's nationalists and industrialists. The utopian ideal that these *"worshippers of the earth"* advance is a world without governments, where the "abusers of the earth" (i.e. free-enterprise capitalists) are reigned in and all the world's resources are protected and controlled for the "benefit of all."[a] With religious zeal, these *"protectors of the earth"* spread the worship of their new-found deity, *"Mother Earth."*

The dubious *"science"* supporting these doomsday claims, and the Marxist political ideology of many of the "environmentalist" leaders (and rank and file collaborators and supporters) not withstanding, these "environmentalists" are given wide latitude and respect in the world's governments and circles of power and influence. Therefore, it seems certain that "environmentalism" will be a main tenet of the Beast's

---

a It is interesting to realize that many of these *"environmentalists"* view the human species as the enemy. They are often found to be zealously pro-abortion, pro-euthanasia, and advancers of the *"human overpopulation myth."*

global religion. And *"environmental zealots"* will assuredly be among the front-line troops[a] that will usher in his one-world government.

The Biblically prophesied one-world religion will be briefly examined in the foregoing chapters. It is interesting to discover that a primary part of the United Nations Charter is devoted to promoting a "religion of man." The primary tenets of this religion include promoting human "self-esteem" and a dictatorial "tolerance" of all peoples and beliefs. This is very similar to the attitude that the Roman Empire took toward the primitive Christian Church. Early Christians were not persecuted and martyred by the Romans because they worshipped Jesus Christ. They were assaulted because they worshipped Him exclusively. They were assured that if they would simply include the emperor in their worship they would be left alone. This same intolerable "tolerance" is perhaps the most sacred doctrine of this humanistic United Nations religion. Everything is to be tolerated but the belief in absolutes and in an absolute God. This dogma will necessarily isolate true believers.

Christ Jesus is the only Savior of men. ***Neither is there salvation in any other: for there is none other name under heaven given among men, whereby we must be saved.**[b]* Yet this exclusivity of the Christian's God is simply an intolerable belief in this age of "tolerance."

What is eminently tolerated, however, is the exaltation of humanity. In the Antichrist, the world will see the ultimate of the human exalting himself above God. The number of the Antichrist is the number of a man,[c] and the deification of man will be the cardinal doctrine of his religious system.

---

a The word, *"troops,"* is used intentionally. The violent propensities of many of these *"protectors of the environment"* is well documented. In recent years many industrial and residential projects in North America and other places have been destroyed by arsonists, who leave charred calling card signatures such as, *"ELF,"* meaning, *"Environmental Liberation Front."*

b Acts 4:12.

c Six hundred sixty-six (666) - See Revelation 13:18.

27: Revealing of the Antichrist

Daniel 8:23-25 - [23]And in the latter time of their kingdom, when the transgressors are come to the full, a king of fierce countenance, and understanding dark sentences, shall stand up. [24]And his power shall be mighty, but not by his own power: and he shall destroy wonderfully, and shall prosper, and practice, and shall destroy the mighty and the holy people. [25]And through his policy also he shall cause craft to prosper in his hand; and he shall magnify himself in his heart, and by peace shall destroy many: he shall also stand up against the Prince of princes; but he shall be broken without hand.

Daniel 9:26-27 - [26]...the people of the prince that shall come shall destroy the city and the sanctuary; and the end thereof shall be with a flood, and unto the end of the war desolations are determined. [27]And he shall confirm the covenant with many for one week: and in the midst of the week he shall cause the sacrifice and the oblation to cease, and for the overspreading of abominations he shall make it desolate, even until the consummation, and that determined shall be poured upon the desolate.

2 Thessalonians 2:3-10 - [3]Let no man deceive you by any means: for that day shall not come, except there come a falling away first, and that man of sin be revealed, the son of perdition; [4]Who opposeth and exalteth himself above all that is called God, or that is worshipped; so that he as God sitteth in the temple of God, showing himself that he is God. [5]Remember ye not, that, when I was yet with you, I told you these things? [6]And now ye know what withholdeth that he might be revealed in his time. [7]For the mystery of iniquity doth already work: only he who now letteth will let, until he be taken out of the way. [8]And then shall that Wicked be revealed, whom the Lord shall consume with the spirit

of his mouth, and shall destroy with the brightness of his coming:
⁹Even him, whose coming is after the working of Satan with all
power and signs and lying wonders, ¹⁰And with all deceivableness
of unrighteousness in them that perish; because they received not
the love of the truth, that they might be saved.

Revelation 13:3-9 - ³And I saw one of his heads as it were wounded to
death; and his deadly wound was healed: and all the world
wondered after the beast. ⁴And they worshipped the dragon which
gave power unto the beast: and they worshipped the beast, saying,
Who is like unto the beast? who is able to make war with him?
⁵And there was given unto him a mouth speaking great things and
blasphemies; and power was given unto him to continue forty and
two months. ⁶And he opened his mouth in blasphemy against
God, to blaspheme his name, and his tabernacle, and them that
dwell in heaven. ⁷And it was given unto him to make war with the
saints, and to overcome them: and power was given him over all
kindreds, and tongues, and nations. ⁸And all that dwell upon the
earth shall worship him, whose names are not written in the book
of life of the Lamb slain from the foundation of the world. ⁹If any
man have an ear, let him hear.

The texts of scripture that describe this Man of Sin declare that he
will be a well-groomed, handsome, charismatic, powerful, and decisive
world leader. From this writer's perspective it is beyond question that
the world is ready to accept just such a person. Many people all over
the world seem to be looking for an attractive leader who will be able
to resolve the most pressing and seemingly "unresolvable" world
problems and tensions. This is especially true of the Arab-Israeli
conflict which is the smouldering tinderbox of the world. Many of
those who have labored over the last several years to seek some
workable resolution to this conflict, testify, *"It seems that only a*
Messiah can resolve this [Arab-Israeli] *conflict."*[a]

---

a This assessment was offered by a "Middle East expert." He posited this
  solution on a political round-table discussion on CNN in 2002.

Christians should be aware that a person matching these very descriptions, who will indeed claim to be Messiah, is prophesied to emerge onto the world scene just before the Lord returns. Given various names or descriptors in Holy Writ, including, *antichrist,*[a] *man of sin, son of perdition,*[b] *king of fierce countenance,*[c] *the prince that shall come,*[d] and *the beast,*[e] it appears that one of this evil being's greatest allurements will be his pragmatic effectiveness in solving world conflicts. With this "gift," and a formidable political power base, he will be propelled on to the world scene. The prophet Daniel revealed that he will spread his corrupting and destructive influence over the earth under the guise of *peace.*[f]

Evidently the accomplishment of this deceiver that will propel him to world prominence, will be his "success" in brokering a peace treaty with multiple parties, including Israel and her mortal enemies. The premier component of this "covenant" will be the promise of world peace.[g] And possibly the most significant ingredient in this world peace will be the "establishment of peace" between Israel and the surrounding Islamic and hostile states. At the joining of this treaty, the seventieth week of Daniel's prophecy will commence.

The consistent Scriptural personality descriptions given of this coming leader include an excessive arrogance[h] and a brazen and blasphemous tongue, most hideously displayed when he sits in the temple and claims that he is Almighty God.[i] These hellish features will come packaged in a talented, handsome, magnetic individual whose outshining "gift" will be the power of oration.

---

a 1 John 2:18, 22, 4:3.

b 2 Thessalonians 2:3.

c Daniel 8:23.

d Daniel 9:26.

e Revelation 11:7, 13:3-4, 17:8, 20:10, and additional references.

f See Daniel 8:25.

g See Daniel 9:26-27.

h See each of the texts at the beginning of this section.

i See Daniel 8:25, 2 Thessalonians 2:4, & Revelation 13:4, 6.

Evidently the Jews will be included among those who initially accept the Messianic claims of this wicked one. During one of the many wearying verbal battles that Jesus endured with the leaders of the Jews, the Lord made an ominous proclamation. He stated, *I am come in my Father's name, and ye receive me not: if another shall come in his own name, him ye will receive.*[a] The irony in the Lord's tearful assessment of His own people should not be overlooked. When the Antichrist comes, the descendants of the very chosen people who rejected their Messiah will receive this Messianic imposter. Thankfully, however, this delusion will be short-lived. As will be discussed further below, the Jews may also be among the first to see through the deception of this pseudo-Messiah.

Apparently the most amazing feat, however, that this *son of perdition*[b] will pull off will be a counterfeit resurrection. The Apostle John reveals that this false Christ will be *wounded to death; and his deadly wound* [will be] *healed: and all the world* [will wonder] *after the beast.*[c] This death and satanic resuscitation of *the beast* will signal the beginning of a devastating persecution of Christians and Jews. It will also mark the likely beginning of a great revival among the Jews. Having been duped by this false Messiah, they will finally realize that the Jewish carpenter's Son from Nazareth was and is their Messiah and will return unto Him. Praise the Lord!

The specter of a satanic reanimation of the Antichrist literally causes the skin to crawl. Evidently it will be Satan himself that will cause this Messianic imposter to "rise from the dead." When this happens the Bible declares that *all the world* [will wonder] *after the beast.*[d] This satanic chicanery will compel a world of self-righteous people to bow down and worship the beast. The Word of God declares that Satan will deceive the men *that dwell on the earth by the means of*

---

a John 5:43.

b 2 Thessalonians 2:3.

c Revelation 13:3.

d Ibid.

those miracles which he had power to do in the sight of the beast; saying to them that dwell on the earth, that they should make an image to the beast, which had the wound by a sword, and did live. And he had power to give life unto the image of the beast, that the image of the beast should both speak, and cause that as many as would not worship the image of the beast should be killed.[a]

The Apostle Paul declared that God Himself will facilitate this deception by sending *strong delusion*[b] on the world's unbelievers. God will do this so *they all might be damned who believed not the truth, but had pleasure in unrighteousness.*[c] It is in this hour that the child of God must humbly cry out to God for discernment of spirits.

The revealing of *the man of sin*[d] is a specific sign that will come to pass before the Lord Jesus Christ returns for His Church. Since Christ expressly warned His disciples to, *Take heed that no man deceive you. For many shall come in my name, saying, I am Christ; and shall deceive many,*[e] Christians would do well to consider this, and be alert!

---

a Revelation 13:14-15.

b 2 Thessalonians 2:11.

c 2 Thessalonians 2:12.

d See 2 Thessalonians 2:1-3.

e Matthew 24:4-5.

28: A Rebuilt Temple

Daniel 9:25-27 - [25]*Know therefore and understand, that from the going forth of the commandment to restore and to build Jerusalem unto the Messiah the Prince shall be seven weeks, and threescore and two weeks: the street shall be built again, and the wall, even in troublous times.* [26]*And after threescore and two weeks shall Messiah be cut off, but not for himself: and the people of the prince that shall come shall destroy the city and the sanctuary; and the end thereof shall be with a flood, and unto the end of the war desolations are determined.* [27]*And he shall confirm the covenant with many for one week: and in the midst of the week he shall cause the sacrifice and the oblation to cease, and for the overspreading of abominations he shall make it desolate, even until the consummation, and that determined shall be poured upon the desolate.*

2 Thessalonians 2:4 - Who opposeth and exalteth himself above all that is called God, or that is worshipped; so that he as God sitteth in the temple of God, showing himself that he is God.

Revelation 11:1-2 - [1]*And there was given me a reed like unto a rod: and the angel stood, saying, Rise, and measure the temple of God, and the altar, and them that worship therein.* [2]*But the court which is without the temple leave out, and measure it not; for it is given unto the Gentiles: and the holy city shall they tread under foot forty and two months.*

These passages describe the existence of a temple that will be in the Holy Land in the last days. The Daniel text infers the presence of a temple and then refers to its desecration by the ***prince that shall come***. This abomination in the temple is the very thing that the Lord Jesus proclaimed would mark the beginning of the Great Tribulation. And

Jesus referred to Daniel's prophecy when describing this desecration.[a] The 2 Thessalonians passage, in describing the abomination the Antichrist will commit that makes the temple desolate, declares quite succinctly that the temple will be in existence when the Man of Sin is revealed. From this reference there is no question that there will be a temple in Israel when the evil one commits his great blasphemy. The Revelation passage describes a temple that is measurable and is in existence in the physical locality of the former temple. The Revelation text is also significant because this passage was penned by the Apostle John after the Romans destroyed the second temple in AD 70.

Though many have tended to allegorize the references to the existence of a rebuilt Jewish temple, or to believe that these prophecies have already been historically realized, it is my considered belief that these prophetic references are literal and their fulfillment, though forthcoming, is yet future. The rebuilding of the temple seems to be directly involved in the covenant that the Antichrist will make with the nation of Israel. It may very well be the "hook" that draws the Jewish state into the treaty.

One implication that can be taken from the Revelation reference included above is that construction of this temple is ongoing or recently completed. The Apostle John is given a measuring rod to take the measurements of the temple, the suggestion being that it is a new structure. The tentative political stability of this building project is also alluded to by the statement, ***But the court which is without the temple leave out, and measure it not; for it is given unto the Gentiles: and the holy city shall they tread under foot forty and two months.***[b]

Here is a possible scenario involving this sign and its connection to the Antichrist-brokered "peace" treaty and the ***abomination of desolation***: This seven year ***covenant*** includes a sanction for the Jews to rebuild the temple. The construction project progresses at an almost miraculous pace, being completed in three and a half years. At the

---

a See Matthew 24:15 & Mark 13:14.

b Revelation 11:2.

official dedication ceremony the Antichrist plays his hand and commits a great abomination which defiles the temple. This abomination? He puts himself forward as the Messiah (*he as God sitteth in the temple of God, showing himself that he is God,*[a]) but the Jews see through the facade. This false Christ, having defiled the temple, is then assassinated by the temple priests. However, three days later this Antichrist reappears, *his deadly wound* [having been] *healed.*[b]

At this point the Christians' Great Tribulation will begin. Christians (both Jew and Gentile) will be hunted down by the armies of this ravenous *beast* and martyred by the millions. Yet, it is in that very dark hour that the promises of Jesus to His beloved will be most precious. His abiding grace and presence will sustain and comfort His children. Following in the path of the faithful martyrs of old, and with rejoicing, His faithful ones will not accept *deliverance; that they might obtain a better resurrection.*[c]

This attack of the satanically reanimated Antichrist is also likely to be the singular event that will spark a great redemption among the Jewish people. In two-thousand years of Church history it has indeed been only a remnant of the chosen people that have accepted their Messiah. Yet, the world awaits a glorious day when salvation will again visit the house of Israel. I believe that it will be at this point when the Israelites will finally see the error of their forefathers and will recognize and worship Christ Jesus their Messiah. So it is again demonstrated that in the darkest hours of man's rebellion against God, the Lord is able to bring forth glorious redemption. Truly the promise of the Lord is sure and steadfast, for *When the enemy shall come in like a flood, the Spirit of the LORD shall lift up a standard against him.*[d]

---

a 2 Thessalonians 2:4.

b Revelation 13:3.

c Hebrews 11:35.

d Isaiah 59:19.

29: Abomination of Desolation

Daniel 9:27 - And he shall confirm the covenant with many for one week: and in the midst of the week he shall cause the sacrifice and the oblation to cease, and for the overspreading of abominations he shall make it desolate, even until the consummation, and that determined shall be poured upon the desolate.

Daniel 9:30-31 - [30] For the ships of Chittim shall come against him: therefore he shall be grieved, and return, and have indignation against the holy covenant: so shall he do; he shall even return, and have intelligence with them that forsake the holy covenant. [31] And arms shall stand on his part, and they shall pollute the sanctuary of strength, and shall take away the daily sacrifice, and they shall place the abomination that maketh desolate.

Daniel 12:11 - And from the time that the daily sacrifice shall be taken away, and the abomination that maketh desolate set up, there shall be a thousand two hundred and ninety days.

Matthew 24:15 - When ye therefore shall see the abomination of desolation, spoken of by Daniel the prophet, stand in the holy place, (whoso readeth, let him understand:)

2 Thessalonians 2:4 - Who opposeth and exalteth himself above all that is called God, or that is worshipped; so that he as God sitteth in the temple of God, showing himself that he is God.

The two preceding signs and this one abound together. This abomination which the Antichrist will commit will desecrate the temple and will signal to the watchful the beginning of the Great Tribulation. This event will occur in the middle of the seven year "peace" *covenant* that the Antichrist will enter into with many nations including the nation of Israel. By a heinous and blasphemous act of desecration, he will defile the temple and cause its desolation. This blasphemy will include a claim by this evil prince that he is Jehovah God.

This is the specific event that Christians are directed to watch for. When it occurs Christians are to flee from the clutches of this wicked one by every means possible. This event will mark the beginning of the Great Tribulation. The first three and one half years of the Tribulation period will be a time of gathering trouble, the second half of this false-peace *covenant* period will be the Great Tribulation. The Scriptures reveal that a great and innumerable multitude of believers will be martyred during that time.[a]

History has recorded two previous abominable desolations of the second temple that stand as foreshadowing events for this final act of abomination. The temple was defiled by a brutal, false-god named, Antiochus IV Epiphanes,[b] a Syrian king (circa 168 BC,) and by Titus, a Roman general (circa AD 70) who also claimed to be a god. In both incidents unclean sacrifices, such as swine flesh, were offered on the altar thus defiling it and causing the sacrificial process to cease until the altar and temple could be cleansed. There was a cleansing that followed the Antiochus IV Epiphanes defilements, but there has not been a restoration and cleansing of the temple since the Titus desecrations.

The third temple, which is yet to be built, will also be defiled by a counterfeit divine. The base character of Antiochus IV Epiphanes seems a fitting foreshadowing of the vicious, bestial, and arrogant nature of the Man of Sin. He will claim to be the God of gods and will defile the temple by word and action. As noted before, the core of this abomination will be his claim to be Jehovah God. He will be the one that ***opposeth and exalteth himself above all that is called God, or that is worshipped; so that he as God sitteth in the temple of God, showing himself that he is God.***[c]

---

a See Revelation 6:9, 7:9-14, 15:2-4, 20:4.

b Antiochus, was the name of thirteen kings of the Seleucid Dynasty. Antiochus IV called himself, *Epiphanes*, meaning "The Shining One," or "(God) Manifest." J. D. Douglas, The New Bible Dictionary, pgs. 41, 42.

c 2 Thessalonians 2:4.

This sign was intended by Jesus to be a very definite indicator of the coming Great Tribulation and His soon return. It is distinguished in the Olivet Discourse as the preeminent sign which would herald the Great Tribulation, and was the particular event to which Christ directed the full attention of His disciples. With that understanding, it follows that Christians of this day should give the most earnest heed to watch for and discern this significant end times event.

30: Mark of the Beast

Revelation 13:16-18 - [16]And he causeth all, both small and great, rich and poor, free and bond, to receive a mark in their right hand, or in their foreheads: [17]And that no man might buy or sell, save he that had the mark, or the name of the beast, or the number of his name. [18]Here is wisdom. Let him that hath understanding count the number of the beast: for it is the number of a man; and his number is Six hundred threescore and six.

Revelation 20:4 - ...I saw the souls of them that were beheaded for the witness of Jesus, and for the word of God, and which had not worshipped the beast, neither his image, <u>neither had received his mark upon their foreheads, or in their hands</u>...

There seems to be some riddle or enigma surrounding this **mark** and **number** of the Beast. It will take persons with wisdom to discern it. Yet it will assuredly be a mark of allegiance. By receiving this hellish mark, people will show their fealty to this false Messiah. This mark of allegiance must also include some sort of identification number, without which people will not be able to **buy or sell.** Evidently there will be an economic system in place that will allow for an ironclad control of the marketplace. Notice that the Bible establishes quite clearly that only those who swear their allegiance to **the beast,** and join his system, will be able to engage in basic economic activity.

In today's super-computer world it is not hard to envision just such a system. Encryption technology is already fully capable of identifying and tracking 100% of a persons cashless financial transactions, and of keeping them distinct from the transactions of the billions of other consumers in the global marketplace. Indeed, it is only in this day that a dictator could exercise such airtight control over his subject's personal financial activities. Consider also, that the location of this mark on a persons body (**in their right hand, or in their foreheads**) could and likely will facilitate laser scanning. The inhabitants of this world are rapidly moving, both in intention and technological ability, toward a super-monitored society. This ability and propensity will be willingly mastered by the Antichrist to facilitate his designs for global domination.

There is a great deal of intrigue surrounding the number *Six hundred threescore and six* (666) mentioned here. Six is identified as the *number of a man*, and, as noted previously, the blasphemous glorification of man. The threefold repetition of a statement or warning in Scripture is often done for emphasis or exaltation. This threefold listing of six could signify the arrogant and emphatic ragings against Almighty God committed by rebellious men and their leader *the son of perdition*. In Psalm 2, the Scripture exposes this rebellious disposition of fallen man with these words, *Why do the heathen rage, and the people imagine a vain thing? The kings of the earth set themselves, and the rulers take counsel together, against the LORD, and against his anointed, saying, Let us break their bands asunder, and cast away their cords from us.*[a]

It is also declared that *Six hundred threescore and six* will identify a specific man, or more precisely, will specifically identify the Antichrist. Numeric values are attached to the letters of the alphabets of both the Hebrew and Greek languages. It may be that the numeric value of the name of this Antichrist will actually equal six-hundred and sixty-six, or it may be that there will be some cryptic connection to this man's name and this number. Whatever the correlation, remember, wise students of Scripture are invited by the Lord to *count the number of the beast.*[b] It should by no means be assumed that it will be easy to make this identification, but the hopeful promise of Scripture is that it will be spiritually possible for the child of God to do so, even in the midst of powerful deception and *strong delusion.*[c]

---

a Psalm 2:1-3.

b Revelation 13:18.

c 2 Thessalonians 2:11.

31: Scoffers

2 Peter 3:3-9 - ³Knowing this first, that there shall come in the last days scoffers, walking after their own lusts, ⁴And saying, Where is the promise of his coming? for since the fathers fell asleep, all things continue as they were from the beginning of the creation. ⁵For this they willingly are ignorant of, that by the word of God the heavens were of old, and the earth standing out of the water and in the water: ⁶Whereby the world that then was, being overflowed with water, perished: ⁷But the heavens and the earth, which are now, by the same word are kept in store, reserved unto fire against the day of judgment and perdition of ungodly men. ⁸But, beloved, be not ignorant of this one thing, that one day is with the Lord as a thousand years, and a thousand years as one day. ⁹The Lord is not slack concerning his promise, as some men count slackness; but is longsuffering to us-ward, not willing that any should perish, but that all should come to repentance.

Though there are many other signs of Christ's coming that could be examined in this text, I felt it appropriate to conclude my survey with this sign of *scoffers*. There is something very intriguing to me about this sign. Simply put, the Bible here declares that in the very last days false teachers and deceiving, lustful leaders will arise in the Church and will scoff at the teaching and mock those who believe that it is the last days and that Christ is coming soon.

Peter reveals three specific signs here which will precede Christ's return. **Sign one**, in the last days scoffers shall rise up in the church specifically denying the soon return of Christ. These scoffers will even go so far as to dismiss as allegorical Scriptural language concerning a second coming of Christ. **Sign two**, Christ's return will continue to seem long delayed from man's point of view, and may take place a thousand years or more from the time of Peter's writing (see verse 8). And **sign three**, God's purpose for "delaying" His return is His merciful patience in allowing the gospel to go forth unto the uttermost part of the earth so that *every kindred, and tongue, and people, and nation*[a] will be represented around the throne in glory[b].

I will not examine in depth the last two signs here, but I do want to focus on this sign of *scoffers*. One consistent characteristic of virtually every generation of Christians since the time of the first apostles is that believers have thought that theirs is the last generation. It seems that in every generation there has been among believers an eager anticipation for Christ's coming, and an irresistible desire to believe that His return will occur in the days of that generation. Many in today's Church criticize this commonly held belief of our Christian forefathers. To many, our spiritual ancestors were overly preoccupied with the return of Christ. They think we need to look to more "relevant matters."

As a Christian who can identify with both the belief in Christ's soon return and the earnest desire for it, I am not very troubled by the eschatological mistakes of my spiritual predecessors. Indeed, I believe that the Holy Spirit is the author of their eager anticipation. I, for one, find a common bond with those Christians of the past that believed that Christ would come in their lifetime. However, what does trouble me in spirit is these professors of Christianity in whom the belief and desire for Christ's return is wanting.

There is, I believe, a Holy Ghost-inspired *earnest expectation*[c] in the heart of the child of God that causes him to long for and expect the *manifestation*[d] of complete redemption. The Apostle Paul defined this *earnest expectation* as an inner *groaning* of the spirit: *ourselves also, which have the firstfruits of the Spirit, even we ourselves groan within ourselves, waiting for the adoption, to wit, the redemption of our body.*[e] Therefore, it should not be surprising that Christians, as a race, are marked with this peculiar expectation. The Holy Spirit has planted this eager desire in the hearts of His beloved.

---

a Revelation 5:9.

b See Chapter 24 for an examination of this sign.

c Romans 8:19.

d Ibid.

e Romans 8:23.

In these days, however, a strange phenomenon is taking place. Suddenly many who claim to be Christians do not have this expectation. With a condescending air, they will even mock those Christians who testify of this expectation. This "Christian intelligentsia" seems to thrive in many pulpits of our churches and behind the lecterns of our Christian colleges and universities. Characteristically they reject the Biblical witness on creation and will opt for Darwin's evolution or some variation of it. They dismiss the Noahic flood as a fairytale. They are numbered among those who impeach the Biblical accounts of the miracles of Christ. So it is not surprising that they scoff at those who believe that Christ is coming soon.

The Apostle Peter gives some key markers to identify these scoffers and to perceive the fulfilment of this sign:

▪ They are in the Church. I believe it necessary to understand that these scoffers will come from within the Church. That is what marks this as a sign of Christ's return. There have always been skeptics among unbelievers that have ridiculed Christians for their faith in Christ and the belief in His promises. But this group will be distinguished from other scoffers because they will emerge from within the Church and will claim that they are believers in Christ. They will even demonstrate a tolerant patronization toward those "fellow believers" who cling to this "simple-minded" belief in Christ's soon return.

▪ They will reject the Biblical account of creation. (*For this they willingly are ignorant of, that by the word of God the heavens were of old, and the earth standing out of the water and in the water.*[a]) The Apostle Peter declared that these *scoffers*, though claiming some understanding of divine creation,[b] will reject (be willingly ignorant of) the Biblical creation story and the description of the antediluvian world. We know this crowd today as the "Theistic Evolution" crowd. They claim to be believers but they reject the report of the One who alone was present at creation; the Lord God Almighty.

---

a 2 Peter 3:5.

b See the end of 2 Peter 3:4.

All Christians should affirm and be convinced that there is no dispute between God and science, or more relevantly, between the Scriptures and science. Science, if it is truly science, will agree with the Scriptures. For the God of science is the God of Scripture. But the Apostle Paul warns us to avoid *oppositions of science falsely so called.*[a] There is no true science that opposes Scripture, but there is a great deal of pseudo-science, or *science falsely so called*, that struts around mocking God and the Scriptures. All this vanity however will soon come to naught! Evolutionary theories, like the sand on the seashore, shift with the wind and tide, but the Scriptures, like an immovable rock, stand fast forever!

▪ They will reject the Biblical account of the global flood. (*For this they willingly are ignorant of, that ...the world that then was, being overflowed with water, perished.*[b]) This willing ignorance of the Noahic flood is particularly important. Creation scholars have noted that there is no greater archeological evidence on the surface of the earth than that there was a recent and global flood. The overwhelming number of fossils and the very existence of the sedimentary strata making up the earth's crust can be explained in no other way. God has left witness in the earth itself that He will judge sin. But these scoffers will be of a particular brazen mold and will flout this evidence turning a blind eye to divine harbingers of moral judgement.

▪ They will deny the verity of a *The Day of the Lord.*[c] (*And saying, Where is the promise of his coming? for since the fathers fell asleep, all things continue as they were from the beginning of the creation.*[d]) The underlying purpose of all the machinations of these scoffers seems to be to deny the reality of eternal judgment. They will be promoters of at least this component of the great apostasy,[e] for they

---

a 1 Timothy 6:20

b 2 Peter 3:5a, 6.

c 2 Peter 3:10. This phrase is used no less than 21 times in the Scripture and refers to the day of God's judgment. For examples see: Isaiah 12:6, 9; Joel 1:15, 2:1, 11; Amos 5:18, 20; 1 Corinthians 5:5; 2 Corinthians 1:14.

d 2 Peter 3:4.

e See Chapter 25.

will contradict the cause-effect connection of iniquity and judgment. It seems that their particular distaste for and rejection of *the day of the Lord*[a] centers around its accompanying judgments for sin. Peter warned that these deceivers will walk *after their own lusts*.[b] So they will naturally want to reject any Christian doctrine that bodes of judgment for sin and puts Biblical restraints on fleshly passions. It is amazing to me how many Christian leaders today lambast the traditional standards of the Church, calling them legalistic, and yet they turn a blind eye to the rising lasciviousness of today's Church. It must be that we are witnessing the rise of lustful scoffers as the apostle foretold.

As was mentioned earlier, finding people in the Church who believe that Jesus is coming soon is not unique. It seems that the majority of Christians of every generation have believed that way. What is strange by historical standards, however, is finding a significant number of professing Christians holding positions of authority in the Church who do not believe that Jesus is coming soon and who demonstrate no desire for Him to come soon. A prevalence of this type of scoffer is the very condition of today's Church!

Therefore, in my estimation, this sign of Christ's soon return is coming to pass today. These "Christians" who deny Christ's soon return, coupled with their embracing of evolution, and their rejection of the Scriptural record of natural history, seem to meet the test of the Scriptural identifiers of the *scoffers* that shall come in the last days. Peter warned that at the time of the end skeptics that deny it is the last days will flourish in the Church. Since we see this happening today, let those of us who *love His appearing*[c] look up with our thoughts on heavenly things and with the precious hope that our *redemption draweth nigh*![d]

---

a 2 Peter 3:10.

b 2 Peter 3:3.

c 2 Timothy 4:8.

d See Luke 21:28.

32: Conclusion

The listing in Part II of expressed signs of Christ's second coming is intended to sharpen the readers awareness of precursory signs in Scripture. There is no claim that this listing is exhaustive! Quite the contrary, there are multitudes of additional signs to be discerningly gleaned from the pages of Holy Writ. Christians are admonished to study the Scriptures and be watchful. Christ's sheep hear His voice and listen to Him. Those same sheep, He will assuredly lead. Therefore, may the Lord's grace keep His Church in the place of diligent watchfulness. Amen!

The Apostle Paul promised that *a crown of righteousness*, given by *the Lord, the righteous judge*, awaits *all... that love his appearing.*[a] The love of His appearing includes a purposed attention to these things. With all the anxiety and woe surrounding the return of Christ it is possible, even likely, that Christians will prefer to avoid these particular matters. But this should not be done. These matters are of great consequence to every Christian, and every diligence should be applied to the gaining of a deeper understanding of them.

The Book of Revelation offers a promise of blessing to everyone *that readeth, and they that hear the words of this prophecy, and keep those things which are written therein: for the time is at hand.*[b] Could it be that the Lord gave this promise as He began the Revelation to counter His followers natural inclination to avoid these anxious subjects? In John the Apostle's concluding salutation he recorded Christ's promise, *Surely I come quickly. Amen.*[c] He then added, *even so, come lord Jesus.*[d] This, *even so*, may not only refer to a desire to see Christ come quickly, but may also refer to a knowledge of the trouble accompanying His return. But the request rests in the certain hope that the troubles accompanying the return of Christ will not be worthy to be compared to the joys of His return. The Apostle Paul put

---

a 2 Timothy 4:8.

b Revelation 1:3.

c Revelation 22:20.

d Ibid.

it this way, *For I reckon that the sufferings of this present time are not worthy to be compared with the glory which shall be revealed in us.*[a]

It is said that a mother forgets all the pain of the birth as soon as she sees the beautiful child she has brought forth. As a man, I cannot relate personally to this remarkable tendency of motherhood, having only experienced the joys of childbirth as a spectator and without its accompanying pain. Yet, it is right to draw a comparison to this tendency of mothers and Christ's return. There will indeed be "birth pains" accompanying the return of Christ, but the beauty of His face will permanently erase all memory of those birth pains in the minds of His beloved Church.

Jesus actually referred to this phenomenon in mothers to describe to His disciples the effects of His return: *A woman when she is in travail hath sorrow, because her hour is come: but as soon as she is delivered of the child, she remembereth no more the anguish, for joy that a man is born into the world. And ye now therefore have sorrow: but I will see you again, and your heart shall rejoice, and your joy no man taketh from you.*[b]

In times like these, may the Lord commend His peace to your heart, the very *peace of God, which passeth all understanding.*[c] This peace alone is able to *keep your hearts and minds through Christ Jesus,*[d] and is the hope and stay for all believers even in the midst of the storm. Hallelujah! May these words of the Lord and Savior Jesus Christ give you hope in this hour: *These things I have spoken unto you, that in me ye might have peace. In the world ye shall have tribulation: but be of good cheer; I have overcome the world.*[e]

The End

---

a Romans 8:18.

b John 16:21-22.

c Philippians 4:7.

d Ibid.

e John 16:33.

Appendix A: Israel's Restoration

Included below are some Scriptural references prophesying the literal restoration of Israel back to the Biblical promised land. These references also describe the apostasy of Israel and prophesy the spiritual salvation of Israel.

Deuteronomy 30:1-5 - ¹And it shall come to pass, when all these things are come upon thee, the blessing and the curse, which I have set before thee, and thou shalt call them to mind among all the nations, whither the LORD thy God hath driven thee, ²And shalt return unto the LORD thy God, and shalt obey his voice according to all that I command thee this day, thou and thy children, with all thine heart, and with all thy soul; ³That then the LORD thy God will turn thy captivity, and have compassion upon thee, and will return and gather thee from all the nations, whither the LORD thy God hath scattered thee. ⁴If any of thine be driven out unto the outmost parts of heaven, from thence will the LORD thy God gather thee, and from thence will he fetch thee: ⁵And the LORD thy God will bring thee into the land which thy fathers possessed, and thou shalt possess it; and he will do thee good, and multiply thee above thy fathers.

Micah 4:1-10 - ¹But in the last days it shall come to pass, that the mountain of the house of the LORD shall be established in the top of the mountains, and it shall be exalted above the hills; and people shall flow unto it. ²And many nations shall come, and say, Come, and let us go up to the mountain of the LORD, and to the house of the God of Jacob; and he will teach us of his ways, and we will walk in his paths: for the law shall go forth of Zion, and the word of the LORD from Jerusalem. ³And he shall judge among many people, and rebuke strong nations afar off; and they shall beat their swords into plowshares, and their spears into pruninghooks: nation shall not lift up a sword against nation, neither shall they learn war any more. ⁴But they shall sit every man under his vine and under his fig tree; and none shall make them afraid: for the mouth of the LORD of hosts hath spoken it. ⁵For all people will walk every one in the name of his god, and we will walk in the name of the LORD our God for ever and ever. ⁶In that day, saith the LORD, will I assemble her that halteth, and I will gather her that is driven out, and her that I have afflicted; ⁷And I will make her that halted a remnant, and her that was cast far off a strong nation: and the LORD shall reign over them in mount Zion from henceforth, even for ever.

⁸And thou, O tower of the flock, the strong hold of the daughter of Zion, unto thee shall it come, even the first dominion; the kingdom shall come to the daughter of Jerusalem. ⁹Now why dost thou cry out aloud? is there no king in thee? is thy counsellor perished? for pangs have taken thee as a woman in travail. ¹⁰Be in pain, and labour to bring forth, O daughter of Zion, like a woman in travail: for now shalt thou go forth out of the city, and thou shalt dwell in the field, and thou shalt go even to Babylon; there shalt thou be delivered; there the LORD shall redeem thee from the hand of thine enemies.

Zephaniah 3:14-20 - ¹⁴Sing, O daughter of Zion; shout, O Israel; be glad and rejoice with all the heart, O daughter of Jerusalem. ¹⁵The LORD hath taken away thy judgments, he hath cast out thine enemy: the king of Israel, even the LORD, is in the midst of thee: thou shalt not see evil any more. ¹⁶In that day it shall be said to Jerusalem, Fear thou not: and to Zion, Let not thine hands be slack. ¹⁷The LORD thy God in the midst of thee is mighty; he will save, he will rejoice over thee with joy; he will rest in his love, he will joy over thee with singing. ¹⁸I will gather them that are sorrowful for the solemn assembly, who are of thee, to whom the reproach of it was a burden. ¹⁹Behold, at that time I will undo all that afflict thee: and I will save her that halteth, and gather her that was driven out; and I will get them praise and fame in every land where they have been put to shame. *²⁰At that time will I bring you again, even in the time that I gather you: for I will make you a name and a praise among all people of the earth, when I turn back your captivity before your eyes, saith the LORD.*

Zechariah 13:1-14:4 - *¹In that day there shall be a fountain opened to the house of David and to the inhabitants of Jerusalem for sin and for uncleanness.* *²And it shall come to pass in that day, saith the LORD of hosts, that I will cut off the names of the idols out of the land, and they shall no more be remembered: and also I will cause the prophets and the unclean spirit to pass out of the land.* *³And it shall come to pass, that when any shall yet prophesy, then his father and his mother that begat him shall say unto him, Thou shalt not live; for thou speakest lies in the name of the LORD: and his father and his mother that begat him shall thrust him through when he prophesieth.* *⁴And it shall come to pass in that day, that the prophets shall be ashamed every one of his vision, when he hath prophesied; neither shall they wear a rough garment to deceive:* *⁵But he shall say, I am no prophet, I am an husbandman; for man taught me to keep cattle from my youth.* *⁶And one shall say unto him, What are these wounds in thine hands? Then he shall answer, Those with which I was wounded in the house of my friends.*

⁷Awake, O sword, against my shepherd, and against the man that is my fellow, saith the LORD of hosts: smite the shepherd, and the sheep shall be scattered: and I will turn mine hand upon the little ones. *⁸And it shall come to pass, that in all the land, saith the LORD, two parts therein shall be cut off and die; but the third shall be left therein.* *⁹And I will bring the third part through the fire, and will refine them as silver is refined, and will try them as gold is tried: they shall call on my name, and I will hear them: I will say, It is my people: and they shall say, The LORD is my God.*

14:1Behold, the day of the LORD cometh, and thy spoil shall be divided in the midst of thee. 2For I will gather all nations against Jerusalem to battle; and the city shall be taken, and the houses rifled, and the women ravished; and half of the city shall go forth into captivity, and the residue of the people shall not be cut off from the city. 3Then shall the LORD go forth, and fight against those nations, as when he fought in the day of battle. 4And his feet shall stand in that day upon the mount of Olives, which is before Jerusalem on the east, and the mount of Olives shall cleave in the midst thereof toward the east and toward the west, and there shall be a very great valley; and half of the mountain shall remove toward the north, and half of it toward the south.

Romans 11:25-32 - 25For I would not, brethren, that ye should be ignorant of this mystery, lest ye should be wise in your own conceits; that blindness in part is happened to Israel, until the fulness of the Gentiles be come in. 26And so all Israel shall be saved: as it is written, There shall come out of Sion the Deliverer, and shall turn away ungodliness from Jacob: 27For this is my covenant unto them, when I shall take away their sins. 28As concerning the gospel, they are enemies for your sakes: but as touching the election, they are beloved for the fathers' sakes. 29For the gifts and calling of God are without repentance. 30For as ye in times past have not believed God, yet have now obtained mercy through their unbelief: 31Even so have these also now not believed, that through your mercy they also may obtain mercy. 32For God hath concluded them all in unbelief, that he might have mercy upon all.

Bibliography:

- Oswald Chambers, <u>My Utmost for His Highest</u>,©1935 Dodd, Mead & Company, Inc., New York; pages sited: 161 (June 9); 314 (Nov. 9).

- J. D. Douglas, <u>The New Bible Dictionary</u>; Wm. B. Eerdmans Publishing Co., Grand Rapids, Michigan; ©1962 Inter-Varsity Fellowship; pages sited: 41, 42.

- Millard J. Erickson, <u>Contemporary Options in Eschatology</u>,©1977 Baker Book House, Grand Rapids, Michigan; pages sited: 154-155, 175.

- Dave Hunt & T. A. McMahon, <u>The Seduction of Christianity</u>,©1985 Harvest House Publishers, Eugene, Oregon; pages sited: 198-201.

- George E. Ladd, <u>The Blessed Hope</u>,©1956 Wm. B. Eerdmans Publishing Co., Grand Rapids, Michigan; page sited: 31.

- James Strong, S.T.D., LL.D., <u>The Greek Dictionary of the New Testament</u>,©1979 Thomas Nelson Publishers, Nashville, Tennessee; pages sited: 14(#602), 15(#646), 33(#2078), 75(#5318-19).

- Dr. Jack Van Impe, <u>Israel's Final Holocaust</u>,©1979 Thomas Nelson Publishers, Nashville, Tennessee; pages sited: 13, 21, 22.

- <u>Webster's New International Dictionary</u>, Second Edition, Unabridged, ©1954 G. & C. Merriam Co.; pages sited: 125, 129, 871, 1245, 1419, & 2063.

General Index:

abomination of desolation . . . *xi,* 12, 89,
. . . . 157, 159

Antichrist . 10-12, 47, 48, 54, 61-62, 64,
. . . . 78, 89, 95, 111-113, 140-141,
. . 150-151, 153-154, 157-159, 163

apocalypse/apocalyptic . . . . *viii, x,* 40

apostasy . 10-12, 78, 116, 145, 167, 171

beast . *xiii,* 12-13, 46-48, 55, 67-68, 148,
. . . . 152-155, 158, 162-163

dispensationism, *et, al* 79-80 87, 90

elect 3-4, 7, 24, 59, 64, 79,
. . . . 90-91, 98, 107, 133

environmentalism 149-150

escape . . . 17, 26-28, 30-35, 57, 113, 140

eschatology/eschatological . *vii-x, xii, xiv,*
. . . . 25, 30-31, 76-77, 110, 165

first resurrection . . . . . *xiii,* 15, 25, 67-70

glorification . . . . . . *xii,* 3, 14-15, 22-25,
. . . . 100, 163

Great Tribulation . *ix-xiii,* 4-5, 9, 13, 15,
. . . 20-21, 24-26, 30-31, 33, 42-53,
. . 56, 58-59, 61, 64, 67-70, 76, 79,
90-92, 111, 130-131, 156, 158-161

imminent/imminence 71-74, 76-78

iniquity 61-63, 65, 100, 113,
. . . . . 116-117, 124-125, 136-137,
. . . . 140-142, 144, 151

Israel . . . . *viii,* 48, 57, 77, 79-86, 88, 90,
. . . . . 100, 104, 111, 115-120, 122,
. . . . . . 153, 157-159, 171-172, 174

last trump 3, 14-15, 22-25

Lot 43, 56, 96-97

Man of Sin 10-12, 61-62, 64, 141,
. . . . 151-153, 155, 157, 160

Marriage Supper of the Lamb . . 9-10, 69

millennial/millennium *xiii-xiv,* 8-10, 19,
. 22-23, 36, 68, 95, 97, 109, 113, 143

mystery 14, 22, 24, 55, 61-63, 65,
. . . . 100-103, 113, 140-141,
. . . . 144, 151, 174

mystery of iniquity 61-63, 65, 113,
. . . . 140-141, 144, 151

Noah/Noe 5, 56, 95, 97, 122, 124

olive tree 82, 84-85

Olivet Discourse . . . 5, 10, 24, 28, 72, 79,
. . . . 87-88, 90-92, 114, 133, 143, 161

posttribulationism, *et, al* . *viii, xii-xiii,* 20,
. . . . . 29, 31, 33-35, 42-43,47, 50, 71,
. . 79, 88, 90, 92, 96-97, 102, 113-114

pretribulationism, *et, al* . . . . . *xii,* 16, 20,
. 22, 27-31, 33, 35-36, 40, 42, 45, 51,
.61-62, 64-65, 71-72, 74, 76-77, 79-80,
87-92, 95-96, 100, 102-103, 110, 114

Rapture . *viii, xi-xiii,* 3-16, 20-21, 23-25,
. . . . . 27-28, 30, 32-36, 40, 42-43, 56,
. . . . . 61-62, 64-72, 74, 76-79, 88-97,
. . . . 100, 102-104, 110-111, 114

resurrection(s) . . . . *viii, x, xiii,* 10, 14-15,
. . . . 23, 25, 66-70, 154, 158

scoffer(s) 128, 164-168

second coming . *vii-xiii,* 1, 12, 16, 22-23,
. . . . 36-41, 79, 87, 97, 107,
. . . . 109, 112, 114, 169

secret   51, 93, 97-98, 101, 103, 136, 148

self love 137-140

Sodom 43, 47-48, 56, 96-97

son of perdition 10, 12, 141, 151,
. . . . 153-154, 163

surprise . . 16-20, 34, 72-73, 93, 118, 131

temple 89, 151, 153, 156-160

thief (in the night) . . 16-21, 40, 72, 75, 164

twinkling of an eye 14, 22, 43

wrath . . . . . . *xii,* 19, 33-34, 42-50, 53-54,
. . . . 56-57, 59, 63, 79, 97, 112

Scripture Index:

Verses Referenced or Quoted: (Each verse is indexed to the page it begins on.)

Old Testament

Genesis 1:9 106
Genesis 3:5-6 141
Genesis 6:11-13 124
Genesis 7:1*ff* 56
Genesis 7:11, 13 56
Genesis 19:15-16 . . . . 43, 56
Genesis 19:24 47-48
Genesis 19:25 48
Genesis 41:25-32 57
Exodus 5:7-9 57
Exodus 6:9 57
Exodus 8:22-23 57
Exodus 9:4, 26 57
Exodus 10:23 57
Exodus 12:10 58
Exodus 12:11 57-58
Exodus 12:12 58
Exodus 12:13 55
Exodus 12:21-23, 27, 43, 48 57
Exodus 16:35 57
Exodus 17:6 57
Leviticus 19:18 138
Deuteronomy 2:7; 8:4; 29:5 58
Deuteronomy 30:1-5 . . . . 116, 171
1 Kings 17:1-24 58
1 Kings 18:39 148
Psalm 2:1-3 163
Psalm 51:5 136
Psalm 78:24-25 57
Psalm 78:30-31 48
Psalm 90:4 . . . . *xiv*
Psalm 91:1-9 51
Psalm 91:10-16 52
Psalm 91:15 . . . . 27, 52
Psalm 93:15 58
Psalm 119:105 . . . . *vii*
Proverbs 6:14, 19 . . . . *viii*
Proverbs 11:8 57
Proverbs 18:24 113
Proverbs 29:1 50
Proverbs 29:5 141
Isaiah 6:7 142
Isaiah 12:6-9 167

Isaiah 14:13-14 141
Isaiah 27:9 117
Isaiah 31:5; 35:1 121
Isaiah 43:2 51
Isaiah 46:9-10 148
Isaiah 51:6 136
Isaiah 53:3-10 39
Isaiah 59:19 158
Isaiah 59:20-21 117
Jeremiah 31:15 94
Jeremiah 32:27 53
Ezekiel 36:16-28 115
Ezekiel 36:29-33 116
Ezekiel 36:24 . . . . 115, 119-120
Ezekiel 36:25-26 . . . . 115, 146
Daniel 3:19-26 58
Daniel 6:22 58
Daniel 8:23 . . . . 151, 153
Daniel 8:24 151
Daniel 8:25 . . . . 151, 153
Daniel 9:2*ff* 120
Daniel 9:25 156
Daniel 9:26 . . . . 151, 153, 156
Daniel 9:27 *xi,* 12, 58, 151, 153,156, 159
Daniel 9:30-31 159
Daniel 10:13, 21 62
Daniel 12:1 62
Daniel 12:4 . . . . 121, 123
Daniel 12:7 . . . . *xi*
Daniel 12:11 . . . . 12, 159
Hosea 2:23 82
Joel 1:15 167
Joel 2:1, 11 167
Joel 2:31 2
Amos 3:7 148
Amos 5:18, 20 167
Micah 4:1-3 . . . . 116, 171
Micah 4:4-10 . . . . 116, 172
Nahum 2:4 121-122
Zephaniah 3:14-19 . . . . 116, 172
Zephaniah 3:20 . . . . 116, 173
Zechariah 13:1-9 . . . . 116, 173
Zechariah 14:1-4 . . . . 116, 174

New Testament

Matthew 2:17-18 94		Matthew 24:43 16,72
Matthew 3:7 43		Matthew 24:44 .... 17, 73
Matthew 4:6 52		Matthew 24:45-51 73
Matthew 5:10 59		Matthew 25:1-13 .... 8, 73
Matthew 7:15 134		Matthew 25:31 .... 34, 37-38
Matthew 7:22-23 137		Matthew 25:32 .... 28, 34, 37, 112
Matthew 11:21-22 48		Matthew 25:33-34 .... 34, 37
Matthew 12:39 41		Matthew 25:35-40 34
Matthew 13:25 3		Matthew 25:41 .... 34, 37
Matthew 13:30 .... 38, 43		Mark 12:31 138
Matthew 13:39 43		Mark 13:7 91
Matthew 16:2-3 71		Mark 13:8 .... 91, 124-125, 127
Matthew 16:18 .... 130, 144		Mark 13:9-13 91
Matthew 19:19 138		Mark 13:14 .... 91, 157
Matthew 22:39 138		Mark 13:15-23 91
Matthew 23:37-51 77		Mark 13:24 .... 4, 91
Matthew 24:1-2 77		Mark 13:25 .... 4, 7, 91
Matthew 24:3 133		Mark 13:26 .... 4, 7, 10, 91
Matthew 24:4 .... 90, 133-134, 155		Mark 13:27 .... 4, 7, 10, 57, 91
Matthew 24:5 .... 90, 155		Mark 13:28-29 91
Matthew 24:6 90		Mark 13:32 73
Matthew 24:7 .... *xi,* 90		Mark 13:33 .... 73, 75
Matthew 24:8 .... 90, 124, 127		Mark 13:34-37 73
Matthew 24:9 ..... *xi,* 90, 129, 131, 144		Mark 16:15 143
Matthew 24:10 .... 90, 129		Luke 3:7 43
Matthew 24:11 .... 90, 133		Luke 4:10-11 52
Matthew 24:12 .... 90, 136-137		Luke 10:3 .... 26, 142, 144
Matthew 24:13 90		Luke 10:21 103
Matthew 24:14 .... 90, 143		Luke 12:37-38 17
Matthew 24:15 .. *xi,* 12, 89-90, 157, 159		Luke 12:39 16-17
Matthew 24:16-19 90		Luke 12:40 17
Matthew 24:20 89-90		Luke 13:19 77
Matthew 24:21 .... *xi,* 90-91, 130		Luke 17:26 .... 95, 124
Matthew 24:22 90		Luke 17: 27 95
Matthew 24:23 .... 90, 98		Luke 17: 28-37 96
Matthew 24:24 .... 90, 133		Luke 21:8 .... 28, 91
Matthew 24:26 .... 90, 97		Luke 21:9-10 91
Matthew 24:27-28 .... 90, 98		Luke 21:11 .... *xi,* 91
Matthew 24:29 ... 3-7, 23-25, 42, 45-46,		Luke 21:12 .... *xi,* 28, 91
.... 56, 64, 91, 95, 97		Luke 21:13-17 .... 28, 91
Matthew 24:30 ... 3, 5, 7, 10, 36, 42, 46,		Luke 21:18 .... 28, 52, 91
.... 64, 74, 91, 106		Luke 21:19-20 .... 28, 91
Matthew 24:31 ... 4, 7, 10, 24, 43, 57,64		Luke 21:23-24 91
.... 91, 107		Luke 21:25 .... *xi,* 91, 124
Matthew 24:36 .... 5, 95		Luke 21:26 .... *xi,* 91
Matthew 24:37 .... 5, 95, 124		Luke 21:27 91
Matthew 24:38-41 .... 5, 95		Luke 21:28 168
Matthew 24:42 .... 16-17, 72, 75		Luke 21:34-36 27

Luke 22:42 142
Luke 24:25-27 . . . . 39, 127
John 1:11 81
John 1:29 39
John 3:5 63
John 3:18 85
John 5:43 154
John 8:31-32 . . . . *vii*
John 15:18-25 77
John 15:20 54
John 16:2 129
John 16:21-22 170
John 16:33 . . . . 26, 53, 59, 170
John 17:15 . . . . 26, 53
John 21:18-19 76
Acts 1:8 . . . . 76, 143, 146
Acts 1:11 . . . . 7, 106
Acts 4:12 . . . . 81, 150
Acts 4:13 104
Acts 4:29 . . . . 27, 35
Acts 9:15 77
Acts 12:6-11 59
Acts 14:22 26
Acts 17:11 134
Acts 21:21 11
Acts 22:15 77
Acts 23:11 77
Acts 26:2 77
Acts 27:24 77
Acts 28:3-5 59
Acts 28:15 7
Romans 1:16 40
Romans 2:28-29 85
Romans 3:2 80
Romans 4:9-16 84
Romans 5:3 26
Romans 5:9 43-44
Romans 5:20 32
Romans 6:1-2 146
Romans 8:9 64
Romans 8:18 170
Romans 8:19 168
Romans 8:23 165
Romans 8:33 4
Romans 9:3, 25-26 82
Romans 9:27 81
Romans 10:19 81
Romans 11:1 . . . . 83, 117
Romans 11:5 . . . . 81, 83
Romans 11:6-7 84

Romans 11:11 . . . . 81, 83
Romans 11:12 83
Romans 11:14 81
Romans 11:15 . . . . 83, 119-120
Romans 11:17 . . . . 82, 84
Romans 11:18 83
Romans 11:20 82
Romans 11:21 83
Romans 11:23 84
Romans 11:24 . . . . 82, 84
Romans 11:25 . . . . 77, 84, 100, 116, 174
Romans 11:26 . 81-82, 84, 116-117, 174
Romans 11:27 . . . . 84, 116-117, 174
Romans 11:28 . . . . 84, 86, 116, 174
Romans 11:29 . . . . 81, 116, 174
Romans 11:30-32 . . . . 116, 174
Romans 13:9 138
Romans 14:11 99
Romans 16:25 100-101
Romans 16:26 101
1 Corinthians 1:7-8 37
1 Corinthians 1:27-31 104
1 Corinthians 2:7 100
1 Corinthians 5:5 167
1 Corinthians 12:3 64
1 Corinthians 13:1-3 137
1 Corinthians 13:9, 12 . . . . *viii*
1 Corinthians 15:51 . . *xii*, 14, 22, 24, 68,
. . . . 100
1 Corinthians 15:52 . . . *xii*, 3, 14-15, 22,
. . . . 24, 43, 68, 100
1 Corinthians 15:53 . . . . *xii*, 22, 100
1 Corinthians 15:54 . . . . . . *xii*, 3, 22, 100
2 Corinthians 1:8-10 59
2 Corinthians 1:14 167
2 Corinthians 4:2 40
2 Corinthians 4:6 105
2 Corinthians 5:10 106
2 Corinthians 9:8 142
2 Corinthians 11:23-27 59
Galatians 3:28 84-85
Galatians 3:29 84-86
Galatians 5:14 138
Ephesians 1:9 100
Ephesians 2:19-21 88
Ephesians 2:22 89
Ephesians 3:1-11 100
Ephesians 4:3 . . . . *vii*
Ephesians 4:13 . . . . *viii*
Ephesians 5:29 139

Ephesians 5:32 100
Ephesians 6:13-18 65
Ephesians 6:19 100
Philippians 1:15-16 137
Philippians 3:8 1
Philippians 3:9 2
Philippians 4:7 170
Colossians 1:18 69
Colossians 1:25-29 100
Colossians 2:1 100
Colossians 3:4 .... 25, 107
Colossians 3:12 4
1 Thessalonians 1:10 43
1 Thessalonians 4:15 .. *xii,* 6, 64, 68, 93
1 Thessalonians 4:16 .. 6, 64, 68, 70, 93
1 Thessalonians 4:17 ... *xii,* 3, 6, 36, 64,
.... 68, 93
1 Thessalonians 5:1 17
1 Thessalonians 5:2 .... 16-17, 126
1 Thessalonians 5:3 17
1 Thessalonians 5:4 16-19
1 Thessalonians 5:5 17
1 Thessalonians 5:6 18
1 Thessalonians 5:9 .... 42, 44
2 Thessalonians 1:3 32
2 Thessalonians 1:4 .... 32, 34
2 Thessalonians 1:5 32
2 Thessalonians 1:6-8 32-33
2 Thessalonians 1:9 33
2 Thessalonians 1:10 33-34
2 Thessalonians 2:1 10, 61, 64, 145, 155
2 Thessalonians 2:2 ..... 10, 13, 61, 64,
.... 145, 155
2 Thessalonians 2:3 . 10, 12, 61, 64, 145,
.... 151, 153-155
2 Thessalonians 2:4 . 151, 156, 158-160
2 Thessalonians 2:5 151
2 Thessalonians 2:6 .... 61, 151
2 Thessalonians 2:7 ... 61, 64, 100, 140
.... 144, 151
2 Thessalonians 2:8 .... 37, 151
2 Thessalonians 2:9-10 152
2 Thessalonians 2:11 .... 155, 163
2 Thessalonians 2:12 155
1 Timothy 3:9 100
1 Timothy 3:16 101
1 Timothy 4:1 .... 11, 145
1 Timothy 6:14 107
1 Timothy 6:20 167
2 Timothy 1:10 107

2 Timothy 2:15 135
2 Timothy 3:1*ff* 145
2 Timothy 3:1 137
2 Timothy 3:2-5 138
2 Timothy 3:12 53
2 Timothy 4:1 107
2 Timothy 4:3-4 11
2 Timothy 4:5*ff* 77
2 Timothy 4:8 .... *vii,* 108, 168-169
Titus 1:1 4
Titus 2:13 108
Hebrews 5:14 .... 78, 134
Hebrews 9:28 108
Hebrews 10:1-4 110
Hebrews 11:7-10, 17-19, 23-28 84
Hebrews 11:35 158
Hebrews 13:5 61
James 1:5 .... *vi,* 104
James 1:6 .... *vi*
James 2:8 138
1 Peter 1:2 4
1 Peter 1:5-6 54
1 Peter 1:7 .... 54, 108
1 Peter 2:22 68
1 Peter 4:17 50
1 Peter 5:4 108
1 Peter 5:8-9 134
2 Peter 1:1 145
2 Peter 1:2-3 .... *vi,* 145
2 Peter 2:4-22 145
2 Peter 3:3 .... 145, 164, 168
2 Peter 3:4 .... 145, 164, 166-167
2 Peter 3:5 .... 164, 166-167
2 Peter 3:6 .... 164, 167
2 Peter 3:7 164
2 Peter 3:8 .... *xiv,* 164
2 Peter 3:9 164
2 Peter 3:10 .... 16, 19, 167-168
1 John 1:1, 13 4
1 John 2:18, 22 153
1 John 2:28 108
1 John 3:2 .... 1, 23, 108
1 John 3:3 .... *xii,* 1
1 John 4:3 153
Jude 1:3 .... *viii*
Jude 1:4 145
Jude 1:9 62
Jude 1:12 48
Jude 1:14-15 .... 42-43, 47, 145
Jude 1:17 145

Jude 1:18 146
Jude 1:24 . . . . *ix,* 26
Jude 1:25 . . . . *ix*
Revelation 1:3 169
Revelation 1:7 . . . *vi,* 42, 93-94, 98, 107
Revelation 1:15 93
Revelation 2:2 134
Revelation 2:13-15 29
Revelation 3:3 . . . . 16, 19
Revelation 3:10 28-31
Revelation 3:11 75
Revelation 4:1 111
Revelation 5:5 85
Revelation 5:9 165
Revelation 6:1-2 63
Revelation 6:3-8 . . . . *xi,* 63
Revelation 6:9 . . . . *xi,* 43, 51, 63,
. . . . 111-112, 160
Revelation 6:10-11 . . . . . *xi,* 43, 63, 112
Revelation 6:12-14 . . . . *xi,* 63
Revelation 6:15 63
Revelation 6:16 . . . . . . *xi,* 42, 48, 50, 63
Revelation 6:17 63
Revelation 7:3 . . . . 54, 112, 120
Revelation 7:4-8 112
Revelation 7:9 . . . . . 43-44, 53, 63, 112,
. . . . 120, 131, 160
Revelation 7:10 . . . 44, 63, 112, 131, 160
Revelation 7:11-12 . . . . 63, 112, 160
Revelation 7:13 43-44, 63, 112, 131, 160
Revelation 7:14 . . . . . 31, 43-44, 54, 63,
. . . . 112, 131, 160
Revelation 8:1-5 . . . . 63, 111
Revelation 8:6-9 63
Revelation 8:10-11 . . . . 63, 128
Revelation 8:12-13 63
Revelation 9:1-3 63
Revelation 9:4 . . . . 55, 63, 112
Revelation 9:5-21 63
Revelation 10:1-6 63
Revelation 10:7 . . . . 24, 63
Revelation 11:1 156
Revelation 11:2 . . . . *xi,* 156-157
Revelation 11:3 . . . . *xi,* 58, 112, 123
Revelation 11:4-6 123
Revelation 11:7 . . . . 123, 153
Revelation 11:8-12 123
Revelation 11:14 . . . . *xi*

Revelation 11:15 63
Revelation 12:6 . . . . *xi,* 58
Revelation 12:7 62
Revelation 12:11 112
Revelation 12:12-13 . . . . *xi*
Revelation 12:17 110
Revelation 13:1-2 . . . . *xi*
Revelation 13:3 . . . . *xi,* 12, 148,
. . . . 152-154, 158
Revelation 13:4 . . . *xi,* 12, 148, 152-153
Revelation 13:5 . . . . *xi,* 152
Revelation 13:6 . . . . *xi,* 152-153
Revelation 13:7 . . . . *xi,* 152
Revelation 13:8 . . . . *xi,* 84, 152
Revelation 13:9 152
Revelation 13:14 154
Revelation 13:15 155
Revelation 13:16-17 . . . . 148, 162
Revelation 13:18 . . . . 150, 162-163
Revelation 14:1-6 . . . . 112, 120
Revelation 14:7-11 112
Revelation 14:12 . . . . 110, 112
Revelation 15:2-4 160
Revelation 15:7 . . . . 47, 63
Revelation 15:8 63
Revelation 16:1 63
Revelation 16:2 . . . . 55, 63
Revelation 16:3-5 63
Revelation 16:6 . . . . 63, 112
Revelation 16:7-14 63
Revelation 16:15 . . . . . . 16, 20-21, 63,
. . . . 75-76, 78
Revelation 16:16-21 63
Revelation 17:8 153
Revelation 18:4 . . . . 55, 112
Revelation 18:24 112
Revelation 19:9 . . . . 9, 69
Revelation 19:10 9
Revelation 19:11-16 . . . . 9, 46
Revelation 19:17-20 46
Revelation 20:4 . . *xiii,* 15, 25, 43, 66, 68,
. . . . 112, 160, 162
Revelation 20:5-6 . . . *xiii,* 15, 25, 67, 69
Revelation 20:10 153
Revelation 20:12-14 68
Revelation 21:7-8 147
Revelation 22:7, 12 75
Revelation 22:20 . . . . 113, 169

www.ingramcontent.com/pod-product-compliance
Lightning Source LLC
LaVergne TN
LVHW011349080426
835511LV00005B/207